For Effie Sanborn Powers and Carolyn Powers Hulstrand

Who shared their love of reading with me,
my siblings, and my cousins:

What a gift their passion for stories,
and for the written word, was to all of us!

Preface

My grandmother grew up around the turn of the twentieth century, in a very small town in the northeastern corner of Iowa. Her formal education ended in the eighth grade, but she always loved to read and write, and she shared this love with her children and grandchildren. She had various jobs both before and after she was married—as a clerk in a jewelry store, a telephone operator, a milliner's assistant, a gift-wrapper in a department store—but for most of her life she worked as a farmer's wife.

My mother grew up on that farm, in northwestern Wisconsin, during the Depression. After high school she went to nursing school in Red Wing, Minnesota, and later she graduated from the University of Minnesota. She too loved to read and write: all her life she tried to write for publication, with little success. After she died, among her papers I found numerous rejections from various magazines, and just one short essay published in the *Minneapolis Star Tribune*—it was about her notoriously bad sense of direction.

In the early 1990s, while going through my mother's papers, I found a few pages from my grandmother's journal, written in 1931. These pages gave me such a vivid peek into her life as a young mother during the Depression that I wanted to find more. I set out on a determined search to find the rest of her journals, which I was pretty sure might be hiding somewhere in my parents' home, in the many boxes of such things my mother had saved.

It has been nearly thirty years since I first began that search—not only for my grandmother's journals, but for my grandmother herself, for an understanding of who she really was. For although I now credit her indirectly for the passion for reading and writing that has made me who I am and has fueled my life's journey, I never felt close to her when she was alive.

Many things have changed in those thirty years. I became a mother; I survived the breakup of my marriage; I moved to France and grew—one might even say blossomed—into a new stage in my life.

While I never did find the journals I so hoped to find—or at least I haven't found them yet—I found a great deal of material that has helped me sketch out as much detail about my grandmother's life, and my mother's, as I can.

Their love of storytelling prepared the way for me to live the adventurous, writerly life I have been fortunate to live. It is their passion for reading, writing, and travel that provided the wind for my sails, a wind that has taken me a long way from Iowa, and from Minnesota, where I grew up.

This, then, is both their story and mine.

Janet Hulstrand
Essoyes (Aube) France
November 2022

Contents

Note to the Reader

This is a memoir, a literary form that tiptoes always—sometimes carefully, sometimes recklessly—along the fault line between fact and fiction. No one's memory is perfect, and everyone has their unique slant on "what happened" at any particular time and place.

I have tried as hard as I can to be honest in this account. A few names have been changed, and certain details have been left out to protect the privacy of some individuals. However, most of the names of the people and places are real.

Prologue

The grandmother who inspired me to write this book is not the one I loved when I was growing up. In fact, it is painful—or is it just kind of embarrassing?—for me to admit it, but I never really liked this grandmother, the Iowa grandmother—my mother's mother—when she was alive.

More precisely, I had figured out all on my own at about the age of ten that she didn't like *me*, and had done the only thing I could think of in retaliation, which was to not like her back.

This was a sad secret I kept to myself, never daring or even wanting to share it with anyone who might've cared—my mother, my sister, or the pack of girl cousins I had grown up with, seven of us close in age, cousins almost as close as sisters, all of whom adored her.

She often gave me and my cousins matching birthday presents. One year she made us all gingham skirts, hand-embroidered in a cross-stitch pattern, in various colors. (Mine was the violet one, and I loved it.) But it was the present she had given me when I was nine or ten that convinced me deep down in my heart that she really didn't like me.

That was the year she gave us the ceramic figurines: they were marked on the bottom with the words "Little Homemaker" and MADE IN JAPAN. Each of the Little Homemakers had a different task: one of them was holding a piece of cake out toward an imaginary guest; another was wiping dishes: a third held a broom; one was stirring something in a mixing bowl, and another was sewing. *They* were all doing something useful: *my* little homemaker was talking on the phone and gazing into the distance. And that is where I got the idea that Grandma thought I talked too much.

She was a rather stern woman, disinclined to tolerate "nonsense" and "sassiness," and I was a lively, imaginative, sometimes willful child with plenty of both sass and nonsense in me, nonsense and sass that frequently spilled out. So the girl on the telephone was only the final bit of evidence I needed to confirm a suspicion I'd harbored for years.

*My cousins and I are in Grandma's kitchen, preparing a play that I've written and conscripted them into. We're having a great time and I am kind of dancing around the room when Grandma appears in the doorway, looking displeased. We're supposed to be cleaning the kitchen (or something), not dancing around the room and preparing a play. She shakes her head, the joy goes out of the room, and we return to the task at hand, chastened. It's all my fault, but I don't feel one bit guilty. I feel annoyed. Isn't life meant for something better than cleaning the kitchen with your cousins? Is the kitchen really so dirty? Isn't **theater** more important?*

The knowledge that my own grandmother didn't like me was a heavy burden, but not nearly as heavy as the burden of knowing I didn't like her. When she died at the age of ninety-two, I was the only one of her sixteen grandchildren not present at her funeral. I didn't have to explain my absence: I was the only one who lived far away, 1200 miles away, in New York City. But since I had traveled the same distance without a moment's hesitation to attend my other grandmother's funeral several years earlier, I knew that when I chose to stay away this time, my mother must have been unable to avoid seeing any longer, by my words and acts of omission if nothing else, that there was something missing in our relationship. That must have been painful for her; she loved her mother very much, and she also loved me. However, she never said a word about it to me.

It wasn't until years later that I began to reassess my relationship with my grandmother. It started shortly after my mom died, as I began to go through her personal papers. One of the first things I found, in a drawer she had dedicated to storing special things, was a file folder in which she had saved cards she'd gotten from us on Mother's Days. In the same folder were a few tiny notebook pages, carefully stored in a plastic sleeve, written in my grandmother's hand. The pages held entries from a journal she had written in 1931, when my mother and her brothers were young children. I opened the pages carefully, heart racing for some reason I didn't understand. Then I read:

> *My babies are growing up. I must write down some of their sayings and doings to help me remember on a lonesome day…We got 100 marbles for 5 cents tonight, and had lots of fun playing marbles after we got home from town. A new phonograph record for Elmer, "The Little Things of Life," and a big bag of overripe bananas to fill up on.*

As I read these words I was transported, with a strong, sympathetic pang I felt as a physical ache, to those days during the Depression when my mother was a little girl in a poor, but happy, family. My grandmother was then a young mother in love with her children, wise enough to know that "a lonesome day" would come, hopeful that capturing the memory of happier times might help her when it did. For the first time I felt the hardness in my heart where she was concerned begin to melt. And I wanted to read more.

I knew there was more, much more. My parents' house was full of boxes of old letters, journals, and other assorted mementos that my mother had saved, both her own and her mother's.

I remembered that my grandmother had always kept a tiny notebook about her, tucked into her apron pocket, and that she would jot things in it in spare moments between doing her household tasks. I knew that if any of those little notebooks had survived, the most likely place they would be stored was in my parents' home, somewhere in the overwhelming piles of stuff.

I set out immediately on a passionate quest to find my grandmother's journals, a quest that lasted several years and involved many hours of discouraging and tedious work, sifting through piles of old papers. I hoped to find many years' worth of diaries; in the end, all I found was a few composition books she had written in as a schoolgirl, a few journals from her later years, and quite a few letters between her and my mother. But that was enough to fuel and guide me in my search for the grandmother I had never really known.

Back to Iowa.

The Journey Begins: Back to Bonair

If we were approaching Bonair from the east and we were about a mile away the first thing we should see would be the top of the elevator and the church steeple. As we come nearer we should see the houses and the white schoolhouse standing apart from the rest of the town...

So began the description my grandmother had written about her hometown in 1907. Fifteen years old at the time, she had gone on to describe the main street of her little town in careful and loving detail, building by building, ending her first entry with a description of the depot of the Chicago, Milwaukee and St. Paul Railway.

A low and rather small building...painted yellow, with brown trimmings...in one corner of the room there is usually a bright fire...Four maps are on the walls and a candy and gum slot machine is in one corner...Throughout the whole building everything will be found neat and in order.

I first read these words—in old-fashioned handwriting, in fading ink—eighty-five years after they were written, sitting in the unfinished attic of the brownstone in Brooklyn where I lived: a long way from small-town Iowa. As I read I felt a sudden rush of connection across the miles and the years—and a growing, and painful, sense of closeness I had never before felt with my grandmother.

As I turned the fragile pages slowly and carefully, I discovered a side of her I had never known. To my surprise, I also found evidence that the mischievous streak I had always felt she had disapproved of in me was not entirely foreign to her own character, as revealed in one of the letters she had written, apparently as an assigned exercise for school:

Dear papa,

Now you know very well, my dear, that I am a very economical girl, but it would certainly cost at the very least one dollar (small sum, indeed) to attend a county fair, and I beg of you to allow me to call your attention to the fact that it would injure my health to remain at home on that notable day when the fair is to be held, so you may observe what an economical turn of mind I have, for doctor bills would certainly amount to more than the named sum. Please forward the required amount at once.

From your dutiful daughter, Effie

As I read on, I began to develop a desire—amorphous, inchoate, but also very strong—to follow the backward trail of my grandmother's life. It was clear from the descriptions in her notebook that Bonair had been a very small town. I didn't know if it even existed anymore, but if it did I wanted to find it, and see what it was like now. Most of all I wanted to learn more about the girl who had become my grandmother.

That summer I had the opportunity to visit Bonair. At first it had seemed that it probably did not even exist any longer: this was pre-Google, and Bonair was not on most maps. But I went to the library, I kept looking, and finally I found it: it was near Cresco, in the northeastern corner of the state. Not too great a detour on the road from Minneapolis, where we would be visiting my dad, to Chicago, where we would be going to see my husband's parents on our way back east. So when we left my dad's house in early August that year, instead of heading southeast from Minneapolis and driving across Wisconsin on the interstate, we dropped straight south and drove on smaller highways, into Iowa.

The Mississippi River valley in northeastern Iowa is hilly, with forested riverbanks and high bluffs. The highway, US 52, curves and dips along through these hills, and it is quiet, peaceful, and beautiful. As we neared Decorah and began to move in a more westerly direction, the land flattened out and we were driving past fields of corn and soybeans. We found our way to Cresco, and from there got directions to Bonair.

Finally the magic moment arrived, when we were able to slowly drive down the main street of what was left of Bonair in 1992, a hundred years after my grandmother was born there.

That evening we approached Bonair from the west, the opposite direction from the one my grandmother had described in her notebook. But no matter which way you came from, there was no church steeple, and no grain elevator. There was no train depot. There was a building on the north side of the street that looked as if it might have been a general store at one time. There were a few houses, some old, some new, and a couple of mobile homes. At the east end of town, where the Methodist church had once stood, in a vacant lot overgrown with weeds there was a church bell mounted on a brick foundation, and a brass plaque that read: "On this site stood the Bonair United Methodist Church. After fulfilling its purpose since 1890, closed with a farewell sermon, June 14, 1987."

The church, too, had been lovingly and painstakingly described in detail by my grandmother in her composition book. Now it was gone, and there was nothing to see there but an empty churchyard returned to prairie, a weathered outhouse, the brick front steps of the church, a silent bell mounted on them, and the brass plaque. Not far from the site where the church had been was a boarded-up, square wooden building that looked like it might have been a one-room schoolhouse. We looked around, then we turned back toward the center of town.

If I had been alone, that probably would have been the end of the day's exploration: I would have been inclined to savor the experience privately, to mull and read, and think and wonder, before returning to Bonair. But my husband is a more outgoing person than I am, and also had the good sense to see that it was silly to have come this far and not take it one step farther. So he knocked on the door of the house that looked like it might have been a general store at one time, and we introduced ourselves to the woman who answered. What felt like a close and personal secret to me at the time, something I felt irrationally should not be spoken of in anything louder than a whisper was, to my husband, exciting news to share: I was in possession of my grandmother's journals! She had written all about this town! She may have lived in this very building!

His enthusiasm was irresistible: the woman invited us inside, and took us into the part of her home that had indeed once been a general store. She showed us the wooden sign she had saved from the train station when the depot was taken down, and my husband took a picture of me holding it.

I told her I was interested in finding out more about the history of the town, and wondered if she knew anything about what Bonair was like long ago. "Oh," she said with a sigh, "No, I don't know much. I come here when everything was gone." She directed us to a neighbor's house, and told us that the man who lived there had been here all his life. Perhaps he could tell us something more about the town.

We followed her directions, and a few minutes later were met at the door by the man's wife, who looked at us warily. She warmed up a little when I explained my mission, but told me that her husband was very sick and couldn't see anyone. I apologized for disturbing them, thanked her, and was turning to leave when she said, "You know, if you want to know about the history of this area, you really ought to go on over to Lime Springs, and talk to Anna May Davis. She's in her eighties, but she's as peppy as anything, and she knows absolutely everything." The woman added that she herself had grown up in Lime Springs, where her father owned a mill, and had moved to Bonair in the 1930s when she married. "I can remember driving through Bonair when I was a girl, and getting quite a thrill," she said. "But by the time I got here most everything was gone."

That was the second time in less than an hour that I had heard almost the exact same words: a refrain of loss.

We drove the seven miles to Lime Springs and found Ms. Davis listed in the local telephone directory. I called her and explained my interest: she invited us to come to her house immediately. As we sat in her living room and I explained what I was interested in learning about, I mentioned that my cousins were all busy creating and raising the next generation of our family, and that it seemed to have fallen to me to research the past. A vibrant woman, indeed "peppy as anything," she went straight to the point. "You have a lot of work to do," she told me, "And there's no time to waste. There are people here you should talk to, but they'll soon be dying!"

A few months later, a major event occurred in our lives: the baby we had been wanting for some years was conceived. I continued to work on uncovering the story of my grandmother and her early life for as long as I could, at long distance, until shortly before his birth: I wrote letters to my mother's cousins, telling them what I was trying to do. I received pictures and letters from them, and from Anna May Davis, pictures that would help me in my search. I carefully filed it all, I kept notes, and I began to write.

Then for a long time, other things took precedence. The first baby was followed by a second. Caring for them filled my days and much of the nights too, and when I wasn't caring for them, I was struggling to contribute to our household income with freelance editorial assignments—or I was asleep, exhausted.

But finally, fourteen years after my first visit there, and with the blessing of my husband and our two boys, now thirteen and ten, I returned to Bonair.

* * *

I arrived there in 2006 without a fixed plan. In fact my going there at all had far more to do with the need for my husband and me to spend some time apart, than my having a clear sense of purpose about my writing. I had been invited to stay in the home of a friend who lived in a lovely river valley in southeastern Minnesota as a place of retreat anytime I wanted to. It seemed like a good time to retreat, so I made a plan to be away for ten days, and bought my plane ticket.

My original thought had been to spend the time I was there reading the old letters I had found stored away in my parents' home when I was hunting for my grandmother's journals, and writing. But I was going to be so close to Bonair, just a couple of hours away. So I decided I would go there with a couple of questions to research, and see where that might lead. I knew, for example, how my grandparents had met (at a box-lunch social), but where was the social held, and when? I knew that my grandmother had grown up in Bonair, and my grandfather somewhere in Iowa, but I had no idea where. I felt sure that by asking a few questions of this nature, and either finding or not finding the answers, a path of further inquiry would open up before me, and I would follow it.

It was a method that worked very well.

* * *

Cresco, Iowa is not far from Mason City, the hometown of Meredith Willson and the prototype for "River City," the fictional town made famous by *The Music Man*. Cresco is the county seat of Howard County, and when I arrived there in the fall of 2006, it struck me as being a model small town. Everything a person could need was there: a clothing store, a grocery store, a gift shop, a Radio Shack, a hardware store, a furniture store. An Italian restaurant, a bakery, a diner. Good public and private schools, a well-equipped and up-to-date library, a local historical society, a community college. Doctors, a dentist, a pharmacy, a veterinarian. A bank, a law office, a post office. There was even a Curves exercise center, where you could work off the pounds gained in eating the caramel rolls they sell in the diner and the bakery. And there were quite a few churches.

Around the corner from the Curves, in the old Opera House, community theater events were being announced, and movies shown. Throughout the downtown area, bronze sculptures celebrating children at play suggested to me that in Cresco people cared about both children and the arts. There was a small, well-tended, vintage-1950s motel on the edge of town, the diner located conveniently nearby. In the town square a historic log cabin and a sculpture of the town's most famous citizen, Norman Borlaug, the "Father of the Green Revolution," winner of the 1970 Nobel Peace Prize, proclaimed the townspeoples' pride in their local heritage.

There were also a couple of things that were noticeably absent: a McDonald's was one of them. Cresco was certainly a large enough community to support such a franchise: the fact that none had been built there yet had to have been due to a decision, whether articulated or not, on the part of the populace. Though I was pretty sure local teenagers would not agree, I felt this was a salutary omission, and surely part of the reason that downtown Cresco was thriving.

It had been a lovely drive there from the place I was staying, near Winona. The road led, at first windingly through the voluptuous bluffs and hills of the river valley, then onto a high plateau, where open sky and fields invited both contemplation and the all too rare opportunity to simply let my mind be still. In an email I sent to my husband that night I attempted to describe it as he, an artist, might see it: "Iowa is beautiful. The drive here was full of gently rolling hills and curving roads, and the palette is of soft, earthy colors and rich textures: green hills, silvery gray sky, rich brown earth turned up in the fields, and the tawny color of dried corn stalks."

I had arrived in Cresco early in the morning, intending to stay only for the day, since I scarcely knew what I was doing there in the first place. I parked the car, and went into the county courthouse, where the volunteer head of the local genealogical society had kindly offered to meet me and show me how to search the public records. Afterward, she led me across the street to the Cresco Public Library, housed in a classic old Carnegie building dedicated in 1915, a build-ing in which surely my grandmother, an avid reader, had spent a fair amount of time as a young woman after she and her family had moved to Cresco.

On a weekday morning in autumn the library was well-used but quiet, and conducive to work. The librarian showed me where the newspaper archives were stored and how to use the microfilm machines. Then he left me alone, letting me know he was there to help me if I needed it.

As soon as I began reading, I found that there was a wealth of information about daily life in the area during the 1890s and the first decades of the twentieth century. Biweekly columns tracked the social life of the town in detail—trips by locals to nearby towns, by auto or rail, were often noted, as were visits from out-of-town friends and family, bridal showers and anniversaries, picnics and other special events. As the pile of photocopied pages beside me grew higher, I could see that there was plenty of information available even on just my own family, and right away I learned some new and interesting things about them. I learned, for example, that the "somewhere in Iowa" my grandfather was from was Kendallville, another hamlet within Cresco's orbit. And after combing through several years' worth of archives I managed to figure out more or less when he and my grandmother had met, though not exactly where.

Still, putting together the pieces of the puzzle that would convey the details and nuances of my grandmother's early life was not going to be easy. I started with a few basic, and rather thin, pieces of information. For example, I knew that she had adored her sister, Ini, who was ten years older than her. Ini had been a milliner in Lime Springs, and several pictures of her and my grandmother together show them wearing some very fine hats. I knew that Ini had died young, leaving behind a husband and a four-year-old daughter. I knew that the daughter had gone to live with my grandparents after Ini's death, and had stayed with them until her father remarried. Why had she not stayed with her father? I wondered. And I wondered even more about Ini and her story as the pile of clips continued to grow.

Before her marriage, Ini had been a rather colorful figure in the social life of Lime Springs and the surrounding area. Ahead of her time, she was a successful businesswoman who went on regular trips by train to Minneapolis, Milwaukee, and Chicago to purchase materials for her shop, and she often took my grandmother with her.

My grandmother (right) and her sister Ini (left)

She apparently knew how to create a popular local business. "A company of ladies spent Saturday afternoon and evening at Ini Sanborn's millinery parlors at Lime Springs," the local paper reported in 1910. "The guests were given a warm reception and the courtesies that had been shown on previous occasions were repeated and appreciated by all. The occasion was a pleasant one." In March of the following year, less than a month after Ini and Evan Griffith, the owner of a livery business in Lime Springs, had eloped, Ini threw another bash for the ladies, this one even more memorable. The local paper reported:

> A company of ladies went [from Bonair] to Lime Springs last Friday to attend Mrs. Griffith's spring millinery opening. The parlors were tastefully decorated and many pretty things in the line of ladies' head-gear were displayed. At 6:00, in company with Mrs. Griffith, all repaired to the Howland Hotel, where a bounteous repast was served and which all enjoyed. The ladies departed on the 9:20 train, thanking the kind hostess who had entertained them so pleasantly.

I learned from reading the newspaper reports that sometime in 1912 Ini Griffith had given birth to her first child. But there was no further mention of the child, not even a name, and I was puzzled when I could find neither a birth certificate nor a death certificate on file in the county courthouse. (Later I was told that this probably meant that the baby had been stillborn.) Around the same time, perhaps not surprisingly, the tone and the nature of the newspaper reports concerning Ini changed.

It may be that her marriage was happy and her new life fulfilling. But I wondered. There were many reports of Ini spending time at her parents' home in Cresco with her second child, a little girl, often for days at a time. About a year before her death, an ad in one of the local papers announced an auction liquidating the stock of her husband's livery business, and the social column noted that he had gone to South Dakota in search of work. "Mrs. Griffith and Marjorie will follow afterward," the report added. But they never made it there. What happened?

I didn't know. And it was partly my growing curiosity about Ini that reminded me there was a world outside to explore as well as the fascinating journey into the past that the newspaper archives were drawing me into. The morning was gone. Reluctantly I pulled myself away from the microfilm machine. I decided to drive out to Bonair again, and on to Lime Springs.

It was a brisk autumn day, beautiful and sunny, with the warm, rich, low-slanting light characteristic of that time of year. As I drove out of Cresco toward Bonair, enjoying the colors of the sky and the rich texture of empty fields recently tilled, my mind emptied and I felt that particular kind of peace that is so hard to achieve in the crowded rush of the day to day, and so easy to at least momentarily achieve when one is released from it, driving on an open road through God's beautiful creation. As I neared Bonair, the classical music station I was listening to began to play Mozart's *Laudate Dominum*, and despite all the things I was worried about on the home front, despite the heavy place in my heart whenever I thought about my faltering marriage, I was filled with an overwhelming sense of happiness and gratitude that I could be here, in this moment, approaching this town that held such meaning and interest for me, hearing this music. "Life is measured in moments," I had once said to my husband, trying to comfort him as he was grappling with his unhappiness over the general direction his life was taking. Here was a moment to be enjoyed, and I enjoyed it.

Bonair was no more filled with activity on that October day than it had been on a warm evening in August when my husband and I had been there together fourteen years earlier. In fact it was even quieter this time, with most children at school and most adults at work. I didn't see anyone. I drove slowly through the town, stopped at the church steps, read the plaque next to the silent church bell again, and was struck with how sad the words on it were. ("How does a church 'fulfill its mission' as long as there are people there to serve?" I thought.) I went to the end of the town near the deserted railroad tracks, and took some pictures. Then I drove on to Lime Springs, for lunch.

The first time I had been in Lime Springs I had commented, somewhat stupidly, on the fact that when I went to buy stamps in the post office, the man behind the counter had asked me where I was from. "How did he know I was from somewhere else?" I asked my husband, and he replied, "Because he knew you weren't from here?"

In the second decade of the twentieth century, when my great-aunt Ini Sanborn had lived there, Lime Springs was a bustling little town full of thriving businesses. It wasn't bustling anymore, and yet it was still a pretty little town, and an amazingly well-equipped one for its size (population about 500). There was a public library open six days a week. There were a couple of restaurants. There was a post office, and an elementary school. I drove slowly around the downtown area, admiring the turn-of-the-century commercial buildings, most of them apparently now used for other things, and wondered if the one that had housed Ini's millinery shop was still standing. I had lunch in a restaurant in a converted industrial building with stamped-tin ceilings. Then I returned to the post office, to ask where Anna May Davis was living.

I had inquired about her in Cresco, and had been surprised to learn that she was still alive—and had recently celebrated her 100th birthday. Some said she was still "doing fine." Others said she "wasn't herself" anymore. (Both statements were probably true.) I assumed she was in a retirement community or nursing home somewhere.

There was a young man working in the post office that day. "She's right up the street, second house on the left," he said, giving me the house number. "You mean she's still living in her *house*?" I asked, incredulous. He smiled a half-smile, and nodded. "By *herself*?" I persisted. He nodded again. "She needs a little help now and then," he said. "And you have to knock hard. She doesn't hear very well."

I drove up the street, parked my car across from the house the post office employee had indicated was her home, and went to the door. I knocked—hard, and loud—and then waited for what seemed like a very long time. Finally the door opened, tentatively. There was a Styrofoam container of what appeared to be a delivery of hot food on the porch; very possibly it was because she was looking for her lunch that she had happened to come to the door, and not because she had heard my knock. I picked up the container and handed it to her. Before I could introduce myself, she asked me who I was representing. "I am representing myself," I said. "I am a writer. You helped me get started on a story I'm writing about my grandmother and I'm back, working on it again."

"I wish I could ask you to stay, but I can't," she said. "I have guests coming." I promised her I wouldn't take much of her time, said I would like to show her some pictures, wondered if she might know any of the people in them. She opened the door for me, and I stepped inside.

But it was not going to work. Her sight wasn't much better than her hearing. I tried writing out on my notepad what I wanted, tried to describe who I was and why I was there, but communication was very difficult, and frustrating for both of us. I quickly decided a simple message was best.

"You helped me get started on a story I'm writing about my grandmother," I nearly shouted in her ear. And simultaneously scribbled, in big block letters I AM A WRITER. YOU HELPED ME. She smiled, and shook her head. "I can't imagine I helped you very much," she demurred. YOU HELPED A LOT. THANK YOU I wrote again.

Then I let myself out, feeling vaguely guilty about being there. Hoping that whoever it was she was expecting would not arrive as I was leaving, and think that I was taking advantage of a vulnerable old woman, invading her privacy, no doubt bringing dangerous germs into the house at the beginning of flu season.

I went back to my car, sighed a deep sigh, and sat there for a while. Then I drove to the cemetery on the edge of town, where Anna May Davis's gravestone was already carved and installed in her family plot, waiting for the chiseling of the missing date.

And there I found the graves of little baby Hugh Griffith, born in 1912, and his mother, my Great-Aunt Ini.

As I stood there reading their names, wondering about Ini's life, looking eastward at the big beautiful sky, the clouds filled with dramatic patterns of shadow and light, I felt the hint of a small, stealthy, but sure sense of peace begin to creep into my soul.

I still didn't know where I was going with my writing; and there were a ton of things I would have liked to know about both Ini and my grandmother that I knew I might not ever be able to find out. My relationship with my husband was in bad shape, and seemed to be getting worse, not better. There were so many problems, big ones, connected to that fact that I had no idea how to solve.

But I knew that coming here had been very important, somehow; and I felt that in doing so I would find the courage and wisdom I needed to move forward not only with my work but with the rest of my life.

I also knew that this place, where I had never lived and had hardly ever even visited was, in a very important sense, home.

Effie Sanborn Powers
(1892-1985)

*"Now that you know how to read,
you'll never have to be bored again."*

A Little Town Called Bonair

The Bonair Train Depot
Photo courtesy of Anna May Davis

In 1892, when my grandmother was born there, Bonair was a town with 30 inhabitants. My great-grandparents, Lewis Philander and Nellie Caroline Sanborn, had moved there not long before from Plymouth Rock, Iowa with their two older girls, Ini and May, aged eight and ten. L. P. Sanborn, as he was known, owned the flour mill.

When my grandmother was seventy-nine years old my mother urged her to write down her recollections of the Bonair of her child-hood. She remembered that in addition to her father's flour mill, there had also been a lumberyard, a grain elevator, and a school about a mile east of the town.

The ones in the town didn't like that so we had a second school upstairs over one of the stores. That was where I started to school, a cracker box, wooden of course, was my desk and Mother brought a small chair for me from home. I was up in the middle grades when they built the schoolhouse.

As the town grew, there were improvements: in 1897, the *Lime Springs Sun* hailed the spanning of Bonair's main street with "an artistic sidewalk of the latest design, by means of which one can now cross the street without wading knee deep in the mud." In that same year the paper reported that L. P. Sanborn had purchased the general store owned by Mr. Webster, and now had "one of the finest residences in the city." My great-grandparents built a new storefront alongside the old store, on the first floor of the house. They turned the old storefront into a living room and bedroom, and now with several extra bedrooms that they didn't use, they could take in boarders. My grandmother recorded the details she remembered:

Mother served meals to anyone coming or going that wanted to eat, so you could say she had a boarding house I suppose. There was Clare Barrett, the depot agent, Harry Dawes, lumber yard, Mike Welch, blacksmith. Then others coming and going. A grain elevator man, a stock buyer. She generally had a table full. As the years went by it seemed that married men had the jobs and she wasn't busy, but the teacher often stayed there, and a student preacher would come from Fayette each weekend and stay there.

L. P. Sanborn had bought his business at a good time: by 1897, the population of Bonair had more than tripled, to 100. There was now a creamery, a dealer of farm implements, two music teachers, a carpenter, a restaurant, a livery, and a barber shop. In addition to running his general and feed store, L. P. Sanborn was the town postmaster. Two years later, in 1899, there would be a new Methodist church, of which my great-grandmother was treasurer, and a school-house on the edge of town, in which "Miss Vinnie Carman handles the birch and teaches the young idea how to shoot," as reported by one of the Cresco newspapers, in an apparent reference to the wide-spread belief of the time that to "spare the rod" was to spoil the child.

While it was at its peak in those days at the turn of the twentieth century, Bonair always had to struggle to survive. News items from the same time period expressed anxiety over the fate of the cream-ery: one, in April of 1897, commented that "If wind were the only thing needful to start a creamery, the one in this city, instead of remaining idle, would be running day and night." A few months later it was noted with relief that the creamery had "at last" been rented, and would soon be put into motion.

I had the general impression from the way my mom had talked about her that Nellie Sanborn, my great-grandmother, was a rather formidable figure, but I wasn't sure if her formidability was on the whole a good or a bad thing. One of the things I found during my research was a newspaper clipping tucked into her personal Bible, about a revival company that had come to town in 1892, the year my grandmother was born. Nellie had carefully recorded, on a piece of paper tucked into the pages of that Bible, the fact that in December 1892, she had "consecrated her life to Christ." The newspaper clip-ping describing the revival preacher, pianist, and singers was next to that. Another note stated that L. P. Sanborn had consecrated *his* life to Christ in 1914. What had happened in the intervening twen-ty-two years, I wondered. How did he hold out for so long? Was it a friendly, or a hostile waiting period? And what was that like for my grandmother as a child?

Clearly Effie, my grandmother, had absorbed an acute sense of right and wrong. One of her school essays, entitled "Sidewalk Education," carefully outlined an argument against people allow-ing their children to run free in the streets of the town, where they would be exposed to "the bad element as well as the good…What can their parents be thinking of to let them do this! and probably the reason is they don't think at all," she wrote. "If asked they will say, 'The children want to play on the street, why not let them?'" and added, "Who does not know that it is easier for a child to learn bad habits than good?"

But her moral stance was not devoid of compassion. She ended her essay on a softer note, asking, "Can we not help this in some way by providing proper ways of amusing them? They are not bad at heart and surely something must be done."

Certainly the prevalence of "solid Christian values" was dominant in the town. One typical entry in the social notes for the *Howard County Times* in 1910 reported on the first in a series of stereopticon lectures, on the Philippines, given at the M.E. Church in Bonair on a Tuesday evening. "The pictures thrown upon the screen were very plain, showing the people and their modes of living, and the great work our country is doing in educating and Christianizing the people in that country," it was reported, adding rather primly, "The lecture was a very interesting one."

In the same issue, an upcoming "box sociable," the type of event at which my grandparents were to meet some time later, was announced. "Each gentleman must bring a box containing lunch enough for two and a slip of paper with his name inside the box," it was explained. "The ladies select the boxes and the gentleman who owns the box is weighed and one-third of a cent per pound is paid for his weight." It ended with a command. "Everybody come and have a good time."

Lectures, chalk-talks, box sociables, and community theater offerings seemed to be the main social events in the small burgs around Howard County, plus in the summer months, Chautauquas. There were also book clubs. One event in 1916 was a debate that took place at the Literary Society in Kendallville. The topic to be debated was "Resolved: That War Causes More Harm in the World

Than Liquor," an interesting choice in the middle of "the Great War," though the US was not yet involved in that war. Whatever the result of the debate in Kendallville that night, however, prohibition did become the law of the land in 1919.

* * *

In 1912, when my grandmother was twenty, her father decided to sell the store in Bonair and move the family to Cresco, the county seat, about seven miles away. "Mr. Sanborn has built up a nice business by honest business methods and we expect the same from Mr. Fiske," the *Howard County Times* noted, adding that the Sanborns planned to move to Cresco, "as soon as a house can be secured." Eventually the house was secured, and the family made the move in 1913.

My great-grandfather probably had seen the writing on the wall. During the years when my grandmother was growing up in Bonair, the only way to get from there to Cresco was by horse and buggy, or by train. That was fine for socializing, and for special excursions, but not for meeting the needs of daily life, which meant that there was plenty of business to be had for businessmen in Bonair. But when Henry Ford began making the first Model T's in 1908 and met with such success, those with a savvy outlook on the future could probably see that little towns like Bonair might not continue to thrive in the same way forever. "He was smart to sell when he did," I said to my ten-year-old son. "Did he sell to someone who wasn't as smart as he was?" he asked, and in the moment I hesitated, trying to think how to answer, he learned something about the harsh realities of the business world.

That first year in Cresco, during the pre-Christmas holiday season, my grandmother worked at the jewelry store in town. She often spent time with her sister Ini and Ini's husband, Evan Griffith, traveling back and forth between Cresco and Lime Springs by train, as she previously had done from Bonair.

In the summer of 1916, when she was twenty-four, she took a train trip to Colorado Springs with a friend, a journey of nearly a thousand miles, apparently mainly for pleasure. I imagine that such a trip was somewhat unusual for young women at the time. She wrote about the journey in one of the tiny pocket notebooks she favored throughout her life, but reading it did not answer some of the main questions I had about the trip. Who were the people she was visiting, and what was the inspiration for it? It seemed to be simply the desire to see another part of the country and to take advantage of the fact that her friend had relatives living there, with whom they could stay. One of the most interesting things to me was a comment she made in her journal about the train trip west. "Our conductor is decidedly Eastern, as were several of the passengers," she wrote. "There is one party from Philadelphia…they are going to Colorado Springs also. I have heard so much good grammar since I left home that I am afraid I will be educated before I get back." I'm not sure what the tone of this remark was meant to be: but reading it, I was reminded of a moment in my own life when I realized I was going to have to either trim back my vocabulary, live with the anti-intellectual comments I was beginning to be teased with, or distance myself from some of my high-school friends. None of those options seemed very appealing to me, but I knew that to deliberately cut off my ability to express myself to the best of my ability was to give up something too precious to lose.

It is also interesting that although my grandmother's mundane comings-and-goings from Bonair to Cresco and back, and her shopping trips with her sister Ini to Milwaukee, Chicago, and Minneapolis, were thoroughly detailed on a regular basis in the social notes of the Lime Spring and Cresco newspapers, there was no mention at all of this unusually adventurous excursion to Colorado. Was it a secret? Hard to imagine, since secrets are very hard to keep in small towns. Was it considered a shame of some kind that was kept out of the papers? Or did some combination of bystander jealousy and disapproval account for the failure to mention this trip?

Much of the activity in the month she stayed in Colorado, at least going by the reports in her diary, was involved in visiting her friend Meda's family, eating "too much" and doing laundry. However, she also experienced some Western-style adventure: she describes a day of riding packhorses into the mountains, and the predictably humorous consequences that resulted. "Well, we went and we are still alive to tell the tale, which is really a little more than I expected," she recorded in her journal the next day. "Our horses arrived here about 8:00 and we were off. The man fixed our stirrups and turned us loose in the cruel world to manage for ourselves…We arrived home at 1 pm having ridden 22 miles…We were so tired we couldn't get to bed fast enough and of course they had all kinds of sport with us about having pillows strapped to us (that was Meda) and about eating our pie standing up (that was Effie)." She concluded, "But we weren't sorry we went anyway."

They returned to Iowa in mid-July, my grandmother noting, "I didn't know how I hated to go 'til it was time to start," and along the way, on the hot, dusty trip back she noted, "I wished a thousand times I was back in Colorado."

A year later, in June of 1917, the *Howard County Times* reported that Effie Sanborn, Meda Black, and Elmer Powers had visited the home of J. L. Powers in Morgan Center. This is the first mention I have been able to find of my grandparents being acquainted.

Elmer Powers was my grandfather, and J. L. Powers was his father. A month later Elmer left for Minneapolis, where he joined the Marines and went on to Philadelphia for training.

There are a great many missing pieces from this part of the story. Though both of my grandparents' names appear now and then in the social columns during the years 1918-20, they are only mentioned together one other time, in November of 1918, when my grandfather was home on leave from Quantico, Virginia, and he and my grandmother spent an afternoon with her sister Ini and Evan Griffith in Lime Springs. Perhaps there was a long-distance courtship via letters during those years. If so, I haven't found it. What I do know is that in February of 1920, when my grandmother was twenty-seven, they married, and moved to central Iowa.

Those were a couple of very eventful years for my grandmother. In November 1918, she hosted a wedding dinner for her younger brother, Phil and his bride. In February 1919, her father died unexpectedly, as he was awaiting a blood transfusion in the hospital in Rochester, Minnesota, home of the Mayo Clinic. "Mr. Sanborn was a man of sterling character," his obituary said. "He was always strictly honest in business and, rather than have any unpleasant words, would always give the other fellow the big end of the bargain....He was also a true friend even to the extent of exposing his own health and convenience in order to help. He was a born optimist and always looked on the bright side of things."

A year later, on February 9, 1920, Effie's beloved sister Ini died, after what her obituary in the local paper described as "a lingering illness." Two weeks after that, on February 25, Effie and Elmer were married at the parsonage of the Methodist church in Cresco. The same day they "boarded the afternoon passenger for Gilman, Iowa," where they were to reside "on a farm near there." Two days later Effie's grandfather, George V. Punteney, celebrated his 100th birthday at the Methodist church in Cresco, a huge local affair that was front-page news in the local paper the following week ("Cresco Man Reaches Century: Citizens Do Honor to a Grand Old Man" the headline said.) There were nearly 300 people there, to honor the pioneer who had as a child floated down the Ohio River from Pittsburgh with his family and later had become one of the founding fathers of Winnieshek County, Iowa.

But Effie wasn't one of them. She had left town two days earlier, for her new life with Elmer. It was February in Iowa, not the busiest time of year for a farmer. Which makes me wonder about Effie's relationship with her grandfather. Did the "grand old man" disapprove of her chosen mate? Had she simply had enough of Cresco by then? Enough that she couldn't wait two more days to get out of there?

How I wish I had wondered about these things much earlier, when she was still alive and able to answer my questions!

On the Banks of the Mississippi

My grandparents on their wedding day, 1920

My grandparents went to Marshall County, in central Iowa, to farm, but they didn't stay there. Perhaps they had read the article in the *Howard County Times* that reported that "a good many farmers" from Iowa and Illinois were arriving in Wisconsin every spring. "Land is climbing up here all the time and cheap land will soon be a thing of the past," the article reported, and added that Wisconsin was "a great place for the dairy cow."

My grandfather couldn't afford to buy his own farm in Iowa: he had been renting land from relatives. So, sometime between March 1920 and March 1924, when their first child was born, my grandparents moved north. And in 1925 they bought fifty-five acres of land in Pierce County, Wisconsin, in the Mississippi River valley, with the intention of starting a dairy farm.

Home births were still the way most babies came into the world, but their first child, Lewis Elmer, my Uncle Lewey, was born in a hospital in Red Wing, Minnesota, across the river, because Effie was expected to have "a hard time" with the birth. And it was indeed a difficult delivery: so difficult, in fact, that my grandfather begged the doctor to "try to save them both, because there won't be any more." Thankfully, the doctor did save them both: and thankfully there were more to come after all: three more, in fact, including my mother, who was born the following year.

It wasn't an easy life, and becoming a farmer's wife involved a lot of learning for my grandmother, a girl who had grown up "in town." "It was kind of a hard adjustment for her," my Uncle Lewey told me. "Her family was kind of well-off and she had to learn to get along with a lot less." I was fifty-three years old when he told me this, and it was the first time I had ever heard mention of any such thing in my life. Whatever sacrifices she may have made to live with my grandfather, whatever accustomed luxuries she may have given up, my grandmother never breathed a word of it to me, or to any of my cousins, that is for sure.

But much later I found a letter she had written to my mom, sometime after Lewey had taken over the farm from my grandparents, which hints (ever-so-obliquely) at how unnatural the life she had chosen to live with my grandfather really was for her. "The most exciting thing that has happened so far this week is the cows got out on the day when Lewis was gone....Some of Lewis's fence washed out is why the cows got out. Lots of bridges are washed out." She concluded, "The country sure is an exciting place."

It was there, in the Mississippi River valley that my mother and her brothers were born, some of them on one side of the river, some on the other. It is not easy to piece together exactly where they lived when, but what is pretty clear is that the farm they had bought, which my grandfather had hoped to be his main source of livelihood, had to be rented out for most of the Depression years.

In 1930, when my mother was four years old, they rented the farm, and moved across the river to Red Wing, Minnesota, where my grandfather got a job in the tannery. His plan was to be gone from the farm for only two years, but it was eight years before he was able to return to farming. During those years, there were several moves back and forth until, as my aunt told me, one day my grandmother just simply "put her foot down" and refused to move again. They must have been living on the farm at that time, for that is where they ended up.

Through those difficult years, when so many farmers lost their farms—according to some reports, about a third of American farmers during the years 1929-1933—my grandparents managed to hang onto theirs, by finding another source of income so they could continue to pay off their loans. And by the time they sold the farm to my Uncle Lewey, in 1949, it had grown to 120 acres.

There is much about my grandmother's life from the time of her marriage to her old age that I know very little about. One intriguing bit I found in the boxes of letters in my parents' home as I was searching for her journals, is a letter she received from her Uncle Vining Sanborn, postmarked Vinton, Louisiana, Sept. 18, 1935.

> *Dear Niece Effie,*
>
> *To begin with I want to thank you for your nice letter and for the photos of your family. You have a fine bunch of kids, sorry that you didn't have one of their father to send me…*
>
> *You seem to want the opinion of a resident of this much abused state at this particular time. Well you put in rather a large order and I can of course only hit a few of the high spots.…*
>
> *Huey Long was an uncommonly able man, an adroit politician whose boyhood dream was to help the masses whom he knew were being exploited by the monied [sic] men at the top and their tools the politicians in their hire…*

The letter goes on to explain in some detail what Huey Long had tried to do, and had done, for the people of Louisiana, and concludes with this summary…"The common people of Louisiana are in mourning. As for me I'm sorry Huey P Long is dead.…" Enclosed with the letter was a handbill titled "The Spirit and Purpose of Huey Long Shall Never Die, Carry On, Comrades, Carry On!" It was signed by Gerald L. K. Smith, Organizer, Share-Our-Wealth Society.

This is one of the few glimpses into my grandmother's life in those years that reveals her continuing intellectual curiosity and engagement with the world outside her own community.

A year later, in August of 1936, she wrote to her mother to say that she and my grandfather were planning a return to their farm.

> *We are planning on moving to our own farm this fall. We are near enough out of debt now so it ought to be easy to make a living. I have had a little experience this year with turkeys and I think I will try to raise more next year. In fact I can almost see*

ahead to where we might be able to have a new house and then I think I would be contented there. You asked if we had spent our bonus. Well we used $400 of it to pay notes etc that we owed and still have $200 worth of the bonds. I think when we wind up our business this fall we will be something ahead. I am wondering if it would be possible to buy back any of those bonds. They would be a good investment. And then again we may not have anything to invest. We had such a nice rain here last night. We are going over to Wisconsin for a ride soon now to see if there is any second crop of hay. It will probably be a good price this year. Love to all from Effie.

But the new house my grandmother was hoping to build was not built until five years later, after Lewey had graduated from high school, in 1941. In the meantime they lived in a house that had holes in the roof, and cracks in the ceiling. One of my uncle's lasting memories of that house was of how they would see snow on the stairs when they would come down into the kitchen on cold winter mornings before going to school.

Just a few years later, Lewey would leave the farm to go to France, where he served in the Battle of the Bulge. I never even knew he had been there until I returned from my first trip to France, and he had asked me how I liked it. "I was there too," he said. For me going to France had been a dream come true. For my uncle it was, as he so elegantly put it, with an amused grin, "not a vacation."

He had not been drafted. When my son Phineas was about twelve, he interviewed Lewey for a school project he was doing, and Lewey explained why he had enlisted. "I wouldn't have had to have gone, but I just thought maybe I should," he said. "See, Hitler, he was gettin' his way with things and y'know, it only takes ten men out of a hundred, to control the other ninety. And if they get control, there isn't a very easy way to stop 'em. And I thought it was time I should help in getting rid of 'em. And I did."

He was in Europe for seventeen months. When he finally sent word to his mother that he was on his way home, she watched the road every day until he was back home, safe again.

My mother's brothers: Jim, Lewey, Dave 1945

The Lonesome Years

There is a big gap in the written record between the time my grandmother was raising her young children in the 1920s and 30s until the 1960s, when she was in her seventies. A few of the letters I found from that period do give a hint, however, that the "lonesome days" she predicted in her 1931 journal did indeed come to pass in the latter part of her life.

My grandparents sold the farm to my Uncle Lewey and Aunt Rose Ann in 1949. After that it's not so clear where they went or what they did. Eventually they ended up living a couple of miles away from the farm, in an old parsonage that was next door to their church, and that is the home they were living in when I was born and throughout my childhood. But there was at least a brief period of time in which they moved to South St. Paul, where my grandfather worked in the Armour meat-packing plant, and my grandmother worked in the gift-wrapping department of the Golden Rule, a St. Paul department store. By then she was fifty-five years old. She took the bus to work, sometimes getting home late at night. For a middle-aged woman who had spent most of her life living either in small towns or in the country, that could not have been much fun. Apparently my mother had written to ask her if she was "blue." Her answer came in a letter postmarked October 21, 1947.

Dear Carol,

It is late but I thought I would write you a line...You asked me if I get blue. I would if I thought this were permanent but I think I will have a home again sometime.... Dad talks quite often about the little farm and when we go there to live, and I think we will in the spring if not before. When we came here [the landlady] told me I could wash in the basement but I hadn't asked before, I took our washing home. But today I gathered up our things and I took them downstairs. She was very much surprised, never thought I would want to wash so much, it would take so much water, and I couldn't use the machine. The outcome is she is going to wash it for me and I will pay her. Oh well.

I got paid today, $42 for two weeks. Ten dollars of it goes for room, $3.36 for bus fare, I don't know how much for eats. I could make more at housework but I guess I will stick to it. They are nice people to work with. If they weren't I couldn't stand it. But they are all nice to me. The old lady here is the only goat-getter. Three times I have come home and the house was all stunk up with fried onions. I wish I had had the nerve to go out in the kitchen and tell her for goodness sake to open the door and get that stink out but you know I couldn't do that. Then other times it has been boiled cabbage or sauerkraut.

We worked til nine tonight and I got home about 10 and it is eleven now so good night, dear. Love from Mother

My Aunt Rose Ann told me, in filling in the background for this period of their lives, that Grandma had followed Grandpa to the city "because he thought that's the way it should be."

How long had it been since she had been able to do something because *she* thought that's the way it should be? I wondered.

I also wondered whether they ever really loved each other.

Sometime after that stint in St. Paul they returned to the country and bought the parsonage next to their church, which was near Lewey's farm. That was probably a bit better for my grandmother, because it was at least a familiar environment, with family close by. But she seems to have still been rather lonely. I did find five years of her diaries, from 1965-69, written when she was in her seventies. It consisted mostly of a litany of daily housekeeping tasks and recordings of social events, but with very little detail of what happened at them. The subdued and infrequent adjectives used to describe her emotional state were just simply sad. These were the words that came up, over and over. "Lonesome. Nervous. Tired." Once, "blue." She never said bored, but she occasionally strongly implied it: "NFO wives talked about butter and ice cream!" in one entry, and in another "I had homemakers here so now my entertaining is done for this year...The lesson was arrangement of furniture. I served chow mein and cake." Once she actually referred to depression. ("Visited B & L & M...I came away very depressed. They have no interests.")

What had happened to the girl from Bonair who loved to read and write, who fantasized about studying at a boarding school in the East, who traveled with her older sister to Minneapolis, Milwaukee, and Chicago, to choose pretty decorations for fancy hats? What had happened even to the young mother, the farmer's wife who wrote to her uncle in Louisiana to ask him what he thought about Huey Long? What had happened to her curiosity, her love of reading? What was she reading now, in her seventies? Had she stopped reading? Or had she just stopped thinking that the reading was important? Had she come to believe that it was not even important enough to mention? Had she forgotten what she had said to each of her children when they learned to read? "Now that you can read you'll never have to be bored again"?

One entry, from September 1968, suggests at least a partial answer to some of these questions. She had just been released from the hospital, where she had gone for some tests. Her first entry after being released reads, "Back in the harness. Baked rolls. Beans on the farm. Canned apples and plums. Have about 52 quarts done. Book Carol sent me—*Peder Victorious* is real good. Rolvaag. I mopped kitchen and porch and cleaned porch windows. Lovely day."

Back in the harness. Did she only get to read when she was in the hospital? Why did she have to continue to work so hard, often at tasks which she apparently wasn't very good at? Like cooking and baking, about which she often commented on her failures, sometimes adding the word "disgusted." Other tasks she frankly despised. ("I keep putting off housework but that is not new," she wrote in June 1968.)

It seems that in the end, her love of reading and writing wasn't enough to allow her to never be bored. But she made sure that her daughter wasn't going to have the same fate.

And she didn't.

CAROLYN POWERS HULSTRAND
(1925-1990)

"YOU COULD BE BETTER THAN YOU ARE,
YOU COULD BE SWINGIN' ON A STAR…"

Carol "Busybus" Powers

Carol "Busybus" Powers with her brothers, c. 1930

The same year my grandparents bought their farm in Pierce County, Wisconsin, my mother was born, on December 10, 1925, near Maiden Rock, a village named for the Native American princess who, local legend told, had thrown herself into the river from a rocky promontory in despair over being forced into a loveless marriage.

The stories I loved most when I was growing up were the bedtime stories my mother told us, about when she was a child. I always pictured these stories as having taken place near the farm in Wisconsin that was still being farmed by my Uncle Lewey when I was growing up. But in fact, many of them must have taken place during the time they were living across the river, in Red Wing.

There was the story about "horse mittens," the time that my two uncles, aged four and six, had slipped away from the house without their mother knowing, and trekked to the one-room schoolhouse where my mother and my Uncle Lewey watched, amazed—(Lewey was amused, my mother *was not)*—as they took the floor at the front of the room, and proudly showed off their most treasured Christmas presents to the class, clapping their hands together in time and announcing boastfully, in unison, "We got GEN-U-INE HORSE HIDE mittens!"

There was the story about how my mother and her brothers had managed to outwit Napoleon, the aggressive gander that terrorized them every day when they returned home from school, grabbing him by the neck ("Up close to his head, so he can't turn around and bite you" my grandmother advised them) and sticking his head into a snowdrift, then making a frantic run for the safety of the house.

There was the time my great-grandmother, "the rady with the rame reg" to my four-year-old mother, who couldn't yet pronounce her l's, made a miraculous recovery as a Midwestern storm approached, scurrying down into the root cellar with the rest of the family, in search of cover. ("It took her a lot longer to get back out," my mother always concluded.)

"Tell us horse mittens!" we would cry. "Tell us about Napoleon!" "Tell us about the rady with the rame reg!" The "rady with the rame reg" was also the one who would bring my inseparable uncles Jim and Dave, the babies of the family, to her side by calling out "Jim-Dave!" "Which one you want Grandma?" one of them would call back. "You both come here, and when you get here I'll tell you which one," was her imperious reply.

As we were always hungry for more, my mother reached as deep as she could into her memory, and pulled out whatever she could to satisfy that hunger. Some of the stories she told were really not stories at all, but wisps of anecdote, or descriptions of local characters. There was Charlie, the hired hand that my Uncle Dave inexplicably referred to as having "dog teeth." There was the neighbor, a recent immigrant from Eastern Europe, who mystified everyone for a time when she referred repeatedly, and excitedly, to the coming of "elekalikaly" to the neighborhood, until they figured out she was referring to electricity. There was my Uncle Dave's way of picking up his boot and banging it on the upstairs bedroom floor in an attempt to make my grandmother, who was below him in the kitchen, believe he was up before he actually was, on those winter mornings when leaving the coziness of his warm bed for the frigid air outside of it was such an unattractive prospect.

Then there was the story of Carol "Busybus" Powers. That was a story about my mother and her father, a man who strongly believed in, and practiced the theory that to "spare the rod" was to spoil the child.

My mother's name was Carolyn Elizabeth Powers. One day when she was about three years old, she was playing outside as her father worked on the roof. Seeing the ladder leaning against the house, she decided it would be fun to climb up, and so she set about doing so, ascending several rungs before my grandfather noticed what she was doing. When he did, he warned her in a stern voice to get back down, right away. "I don't have to get down," she called up to him. "I'm Carol Busybus Powers!" "You'd better get down, and right now," was his reply. And knowing that physical punishment was being threatened, she did.

I loved that story because to me it represented a spirit of adventure and independence I believed my mother must have had before much of it was beaten out of her. I did not think of my mother as being a very adventurous person. To me Amelia Earhart was an adventurous woman. Nineteenth-century women writers, like Julia Ward Howe and Harriet Beecher Stowe, whose biographies I devoured in the Childhood of Famous American Series, were my heroines. And also, especially after the assassination of President Kennedy, Jacqueline Kennedy, whose glamorous life and gracious style fueled the direction of my dreams, and provided me with a role model distinctly different from the one provided by my own mother.

My mom, on the other hand, was "just" a nurse, and a mom. When I was young, I didn't know how much courage, initiative, and determination it had taken for her to get herself out of the farming community where she had grown up to the suburbs of St. Paul, where we lived for the first few years of my life. I didn't know that from her teen years she had ventured much farther out into the world than most people where she came from: working as a maid for a summer at a resort hotel in Yellowstone Park, signing up as a cadet nurse during the war, working as a nurse during the polio epidemic. I didn't know that a spirit of adventure had also been required for her to meet with enthusiasm the prospect of moving our family "out East" to Ohio, leaving all her friends and family behind, which we did when I was five years old, so that my father could take part in one of the greatest adventures of the twentieth century: the Apollo project, which took man to the moon.

After she died and I was sorting it all out, I began to realize how far she had ventured out from the safety and comfort of her world. One day she had told me about a boyfriend she had had before she knew my father. He had wanted to marry her, but she had declined.

In going through her papers, I found a letter this beau had written to her:

> …*Carol, dear, you tell me to not get serious. Honey I just can't help being serious about you. I think I fell I love with you that first nite I saw you at graduation. Since then I haven't been able to get you out of my mind for a moment. If I hadn't been to graduation that nite I probably might never have gotten to know you. I'm glad I was there. You weren't really serious about seeing all those far off places are you? If you are, tho, you have my best*

wishes wherever your travels may take you. I do very much wish you were going to stay around here tho…

My mom was indeed very serious about seeing "all those far-off places." She traveled far and frequently by bus, across the western half of the United States several times in the years before she was married; it was her idea that she and my dad should go to Mexico on their honeymoon; they came to visit me several times when I was living in New York, and she loved being there; and toward the end of her life my parents made it as far as Israel, Syria, Jordan, and China. "Bill was nice," my mom had told me. "He was very nice. But he wasn't going anywhere…"

One of the songs she often sang to us at bedtime included the line *"You could be better than you are…you could be swingin' on a star…"*

My mom wanted to be better than she was, and she wanted to go somewhere.

And with my dad, she did.

Carolyn Powers, R.N.

For women of my mother's generation and social class, there were basically two career paths, or at least two *typical* professional career paths: nursing, and teaching.

My mother chose to be a nurse. Why?

This is a question I never asked her, and never even really wondered about until I was writing this book. Then it occurred to me to wonder why someone who loved writing and reading as much as she did would choose to be a nurse rather than a teacher. Especially since for almost the last half of her career she preferred teaching student nurses to working as a nurse herself.

So I asked my aunt, who had been her roommate in nursing school, if she knew why. "I think for her that was the best opportunity for her to have a profession, and a way to make money," my aunt said. "There was no college in Red Wing then, but there was a nursing school at the hospital. It wasn't too far away from home, and it didn't cost as much as going to college. She worked as a nurse's aide first, to see if she would like it. And I guess she liked it well enough."

"I guess she liked it well enough." In other words, she took the only path that was readily open to her, and that would allow her to become an independent woman.

I'm pretty sure it was not passion that caused her to follow this path, though she did have a strong interest in psychiatric nursing, and some of her best work-related stories came from what was still called back then by some "the insane asylum," or, more politely, "the state hospital." I asked her to tell me these stories over and over, and I always wished there were more of them. She probably did too.

Though it may not have been out of passion that she chose nursing, I think she always appreciated the independence it gave her. She often pointed out to me that one of the best things about nursing was the diversity of opportunities available within the profession— and she always mentioned "home health care" and "public health nursing" as two of those opportunities.

She was a "working mom" in a time when it wouldn't have been necessary for her to be one: it was the 1950s and 60s, and my dad had a good job as an electronics engineer. I thought it was a little bit inconsiderate of her to take up part-time nursing again when she did, mainly because she left me at the age of fourteen or so with the responsibility of preparing evening meals for the family several nights a week. But looking back I realize that this act conveyed a very important and powerful message: family is important, but so are the independent activities of each member of the family. Also, it is possible to juggle family and career in such a way that both are fulfilled, and neither is harmed. Also, fourteen-year-old girls are old enough to make a meaningful contribution to the functioning of the family. I learned later that this was actually not the first time she had gone back to work after I was born. She had worked the overnight shift, part-time also, for a while when I was a baby, so she must not have *hated* nursing. Then she took off quite a few years to just be at home with us.

She had started nursing school in 1943, at the precise moment when the federal government, through the Public Health Service, was establishing the US Cadet Nurse Corps as a way of dealing with a nursing shortage caused by World War II. This was very fortuitous timing, since the program subsidized the cost of nursing school. After she graduated, both she and my aunt worked at Gillette Hospital in St. Paul for an American Red Cross program for polio victims. "At that time the highest wage for private duty nursing was $10 for an eight-hour shift," my aunt said. "And that is what we got working for the American Red Cross."

So, I think nursing was the ticket to the kind of life she wanted—independent and professional. But I also think that on some level it was never easy, or natural, for her. I don't think it was really the best fit.

When we were in our teens, one day my cousin Brenda announced that she was thinking about becoming a nurse. My mom hooted with laughter—"YOU?!" she said—which I thought was kind of rude, and which insulted my cousin and hurt her feelings. I imagine that my cousin's mom, who was also a nurse, must have found a way to convince my cousin—who did in fact become a nurse, and a very good and happy one—not to either take the laughter to heart, or hold it against my mom.

But it wasn't until many years later, when I had the conversation with my aunt about why my mom had chosen nursing, that I began to have some idea why she might have had that reaction.

My cousin was my first coauthor. She and I had even published a play we wrote together, in a children's magazine. So perhaps my mom, on some very fundamental level, was thinking of my cousin as a writer. And on some very fundamental level I think she also might have thought, "Why would anyone with literary interests want to become a nurse? Unless she had no other choice."

The thought was, apparently, to my mother, laughable.

A Hankering to See the World

In the years before my mother was married, she traveled as much as she could. She made several trips by bus as far as California. She described one of them in an early letter she wrote to my dad, in July of 1947, when she was twenty-one years old. It was probably the first letter she wrote to him, since she signed it "Carol, your acquaintance through Rosy." ("Rosy" was her nursing school roommate.)

She begins by explaining that she had taken two weeks of vacation "without pay," which would have been a significant fact for her. And she continues…

…I certainly made the most of my time. I went to California—took the central route through Iowa, Nebraska (horrible state), Utah (beautiful in spite of the desert) the red mountains were beautiful. We stopped at Salt Lake City for an hour and I got a glimpse of the Mormon church. Then through Nevada and up California through L.A., to a small town of Paso Robles. I went out with a girlfriend and we stayed with her sister. The ocean was glorious I thought…By then it was time to come home again. My girlfriend is a school teacher so is staying all summer. I came back the northern route—San Francisco, Portland, Seattle, Spokane, Butte, Billings, and Dakota. How I love travel—and the interesting people you meet. I could write a book but don't imagine anyone would read it. I went both ways by Greyhound RT ticket was only $67. I didn't think that was bad at all. I certainly saw a lot.

In this letter three things stand out to me: one, her love of travel. Two, her desire to write a book. Three, her doubt that anyone would want to read it.

And yet she wrote. When she was back on hospital duty that same summer she wrote an interesting set of observations one night during an evening shift she was working. She apparently was on the "psych" ward that night. I realized to my chagrin while reading, that the "mean" nurse she refers to was none other than herself. Interestingly, the first paragraph was crossed out, though left perfectly legible. Is this because she herself realized that she really *was* being mean?

SOUNDS IN A HOSPITAL

There is a man upstairs chuckling heavily. There is also a 14-year-old girl not 10 feet from me crying her heart out because she can't have her mother. She begs and pleads to no avail. She got a "meanie" for a nurse tonight who will not humor her. What makes children so spoiled. Pampering with money, not making them accept responsibilities and realities as they grow up or just plain babying them.

Footsteps of a nurse, light and free, coming to work. 8 hours from now they will be heavy, slow and will drag according to how much they were called upon to serve during the night.

A lusty snore edges in and comes above all other noises. Sounds like my father—almost.

The 11:00 streetcar just went by with a late load of lonely passengers.

A cough—how common and annoying.

The buzz of an electric fan tells us it has been a very hot day and people are still trying to cool off.

The cars going by outside to the nearby park where they can view the entire city from above. How quiet and peaceful it looks at night up above and a few miles away. (The river, the highway, the railroad and airport)

A new noise comes to my ear—charts being placed and replaced as nurses note the condition of their patients.

Even the mosquito must add his buzz to the multitude of sounds.

The train lumbers on carrying her passengers to their destinations—the weary, the eager, the old, the young, the patient and impatient, travelers all and with a common destiny.

The whispering nurses tiptoeing on duty have come to relieve this girl who will now lay down her pen and give them a report on what each has done since last they saw them.

Thoughts while showering:

Think of the money our nervous patients pay out to come here and be told what to do and what not to do.

Big men who once held responsible positions happy because they are getting over a depression and can actually throw a ball back and forth and get fun out of it.

Women, middle-aged, whose families have given up, crocheting doll dresses one after another because for a period of a few months their grave responsibilities have been taken from them, or because they left them when the strain became too strong.

I'm not sure exactly where the lack of sympathy she had for some of her patients came from: maybe from the strict, self-righteous Puritanical world she grew up in? So prone to judgment, so strangely lacking in compassion. I think part of it was also a rather harsh class anger. She clearly felt a resentment toward privileged people to the degree that the resentment could cause her to suppress a natural feeling of sympathy for a child of fourteen separated from her mother, lying in a hospital bed, crying.

Reading this made me sad.

During the summer of 1949, when she was twenty-three, she and a friend went to work as chambermaids in a fancy hotel in Yellowstone National Park. The class resentment, or in this case perhaps merely disdain, came through in one of her remarks recorded there too. She talks about turning down beds for Bob Hope and his family, and says of them that they seemed "quite ordinary."

This was right after she had graduated from the University of Minnesota. When her father found out she was going to be a chambermaid for the summer he had "hooted" ("All that schooling for this?!") My mother's response to this remark, in a letter she wrote to my father was, "But...I've seen so little of this country and I feel like it's now or never..."

As it turned out, it was *not* "now or never." She was going to see quite a bit of the world during her life. Because she married my dad, and he was willing to follow—or to lead—her pretty much wherever she wanted to go.

My parents, late 1940s

"It's so nice being with you, Carol"

My parents' correspondence had begun in 1947, when he was stationed at an Army post in Japan working as an X-ray technician, and she was about to begin studying for her nursing degree at the University of Minnesota. When my dad returned from Japan he lived for a time with his parents on their farm near Cannon Falls, Minnesota. Later, like a "good Swedish-American boy," he started college at Gustavus Adolphus College, but fairly quickly he pronounced it "a country club" and transferred to the University of Minnesota in Minneapolis, to study electrical engineering.

Once he was back stateside, he and my mom began dating, but they continued to write to each other frequently as well. At that time long-distance telephoning was very expensive, and the postal service was inexpensive, quick, and highly reliable, which is clear in the fact that they were able to count on making arrangements to meet each other on weekends—in Red Wing, Zumbrota, or Cannon Falls—through the mail.

At first, and for quite a long time, my dad signed his letters "Bye for now, Bert." Then, in 1949, nearly two years after their correspondence had begun, he suddenly closed one of his letters with the word "Love." A couple of months later she signed one of her letters by saying "...I don't know why I missed you so much this weekend but I did. I said it and I'm glad. Love, Carol." That seems to be the first time she used the word "love" in signing off.

As their relationship became more serious, he started closing almost every letter—all of the ones that followed a weekend they had spent together—with the words "It's so nice being with you,

Carol." From the beginning he adored her, and he never failed to let her know that he did.

Their relationship did seem to hit a bit of a snag sometime a few years in. In February of 1950 she wrote about it in her diary.

> *I told Bert that I didn't think I would ever marry him. We both felt badly and don't want to call it quits entirely so are going to the game Monday night and will plan to go to see George & Mabel [his brother and sister-in-law] next weekend.*

Obviously her feelings about him must have been somewhat ambivalent. But she did start dating someone else at that time, who she described as "a nice guy who is a good student in Chemistry."

It's not clear from her cryptic, or at least not very expansive, remarks what the problem had been with my dad, but I suspect different views about religion might have been at least part of it. With the "new guy" she writes about having "a very nice time," but mentions friction over religious topics with him. "The subject of predestination and free will not answered," she notes after one of their dates, and following her next date with him she wrote that they had "a real nice time. It was the first time I had seen a hockey game. Religion was not discussed…"

A few weeks later she went to the Ice Capades with my dad. "We had a very nice time," she noted, and added, "No arguments or discussions."

A couple of months later she wrote "I've been trying to break up with Bert but just don't seem to get around to it. We do have lots of fun together…." And by June of 1950, they seem to have been settling into a new phase of their relationship.

My mother had by now graduated from the university with her nursing degree, and had a job teaching student nurses at the state hospital in Rochester, Minnesota, while my father was continuing to study engineering at the university in Minneapolis. That month she wrote to him, saying, "I like my work better and better all the time. The students are so nice and the aides are interesting too. It constantly amazes me to think that I can teach people things that are new to them. Another thing that is nice about my work is that I get to work in every part of the hospital, not just on one ward."

On June 27 of that year, she wrote, "Bert, I think you understand me better almost better than I understand myself. I am so hard to understand at times. I know it must take a lot of patience and I appreciate it..."

It was still almost two years before they married, and clearly, whether because she demanded it, or because they both believed it was a necessary prerequisite to marrying, his getting a job first was, in both of their minds, a requirement. But by the time he was looking for a job, they were functioning as a couple: he reporting to her on his job interviews in Chicago, Cedar Rapids, and New Jersey, she adding her thoughts about each, and giving her approval, even for a move to the East Coast, which would involve taking them such a great distance from home and family.

Finally, in January of 1952, with his first engineering job secured—at Honeywell, in a suburb of St. Paul—my parents were married by my mom's Uncle Maurice, who was a minister in a small town in Illinois. It was a very small wedding, with some members of the family there, and some absent, probably due to the long distance from home, combined with the January date and the unreliability of travel during the winter. They took a wedding trip to Mexico, then returned to St. Paul, where they had rented an apartment.

Then they lived "happily ever after" until my mom died thirty-eight years later, with my father by her side, holding her hand. Right after she died, he said to us, voice breaking, through his tears. "She taught us how to live, and now she has taught us how to die."

And though he soldiered on admirably without her for fourteen years, he never got over missing her, and he was rarely able to speak of her without tears in his eyes, and a catch in his throat.

* * *

Although I did not spend very much time thinking about it, I did wonder a bit from time to time what had attracted my dad to my mom. It was easy to see what she saw in him: someone with whom she could discuss interesting topics, even if they didn't always agree. Someone who loved her and accepted her for who she was with no reservations, even about her not very good—okay, *really* not good—cooking. Someone who was hard-working, intelligent, kind, and who was willing to follow her around the world as she continued to try to see more of it.

She was not nearly as intellectual as he was, but she was always intellectually curious. Perhaps it was that that he valued in her, I thought. Or maybe the way she was always so candid and fearless in expressing her idiosyncratic, offbeat opinions about things. (Opinions that often caused me to roll my eyes, but which never caused him to roll his, though he sometimes smiled bemusedly at some of the things she said.)

In any case, while it was not quite clear to me what he saw in her, it was abundantly clear that they were very happy together.

Then, while I was preparing the final manuscript of this book, I found something he had mailed to me four days before he died that I had forgotten about. "Just a few things I think you should know about Carolyn" was typed on the top of the page. What followed was a chronology of the important events of her life: where she was educated, the various nursing jobs she had held, and details about some of the foster children she had taken into our home and cared for when my brother and I were small, and again after we had grown up and left home. At the end of the chronology he wrote:

Carolyn was always glad to try new things. After a short career as a contract nurse she taught practical nursing at Anoka Hennepin District 11. As an LPN teacher she was part of a committee that rewrote the LPN tests for graduation. She spent the last 19 years of her life working at the Hennepin County Correction facility. It gave her a chance to see a new type of people up close for an extended time. It may have been the new challenges, or the increased support staff, or the very good benefit program, or the lakeside setting of the facility. It may have been the hours, two shifts only: 7-3 and 3-11. She also continued her foster care work....

And he concluded with these words:

Carolyn's goal in life was to help people and I am the people that she helped most of all. I thank God that I knew her and that we were married for 38 years and that I have two daughters that look very much like her and a son that looks a lot like a Powers.

Mothers and Daughters

Every day, every hour, every minute, every second of the day, in every way, I will try, I will try, I will try, to be more like my mother. By Carol and from Carol.

That is the text of a homemade valentine my mother made in 1935, when she was nine, for her mother.

I was not the kind of daughter my mother had been. Our relationship from the very beginning was, though close, also frequently conflictual. "Janet and I had a good week. A couple of minor blow-ups but we make up fast so I guess our love will conquer all..." she wrote to her mother in 1968, when I was fifteen.

By the time I was seventeen, things had gotten rougher: "Janet and I seem to fight about almost everything it seems...hope it won't be like that with Betsey," she wrote in her diary the year I graduated from high school.

How old was I when she told me to stand still while she hit my rear end with a hairbrush? I don't know. Too old for that kind of thing, if ever there is a time when it's okay. (I do not believe there is.) Was it the same time I had screamed in her face that I hated her? My anger was so intense that time that it frightened me: it stripped my voice raw, and made me feel like my head was about to explode. "You're acting like some of the patients at the state hospital," she said, calmly enough, and although that was probably true, what kind of a thing was that to say to her daughter? Why did she say it? Why did she push me away like that?

And how did we get through to the other side of these horrific pitched mother/daughter battles?

I think it was the depth and the strength of her love for me (the "love that conquers all" that she mentioned to her mother) that saved us. And in my twenties we finally made our peace with each other.

There were a couple of incidents that marked this passage. One was when I was preparing to move from one communal household in Minneapolis, in a not very safe neighborhood, to another one in a very safe and pleasant neighborhood. I think I was about twenty-three at the time. The problem for my mother was that in the new household I would be the only young woman. It was a group of boys I had known in high school, mainly, living there. My mom thought it was not a good situation for a young woman to be living in a house of all young men.

I can see why she felt this way, given her upbringing, and the general beliefs of her generation. But though I would have loved to have been "shacking up" with one of the young men in that house, alas there was no such chance. The one I was in love with wasn't interested in me at all.

At one point I proposed moving a chest of drawers I had borrowed from my parents' home from the house I was living in to the new house. My mother said that if I moved into that house, I had to return the chest of drawers to them, because she did not approve of my moving there.

I said that if she insisted, I would bring it back home. And then I would take *my* chest of drawers (which was still in their home) to the new place. But, I pointed out, that would be an awful lot of trucking chests of drawers around for little effect.

She saw the logic in this argument, and she was always quite practical. I guess she must have also seen that I was not going to change my mind. And she relented.

A few years later when I was indeed "living in sin" with my future husband, there was another obstacle for us to surmount. The advice columnist Dear Abby had convinced the parents of baby boomers that they certainly didn't have to tolerate immoral behavior under their own roofs. She advised them to tell their promiscuous offspring that they had a policy of "Our house, our rules." This came between us for a while, but eventually my mom's love for me won out again.

Because of the Dear Abby doctrine, we stay with friends in Minneapolis instead of with my parents in Coon Rapids when we're in Minnesota. One day I tell Mom we will stay in a motel near their house that night so we can see them early the next day. She pauses, looks uncomfortable, avoids eye contact with me. Then she says, a bit meekly, almost mumbles, "You can stay here if you like." As I pause, trying to think what she means exactly, and what I should say in reply, she adds, "Well, I mean, that's why you're not staying here, isn't it?" Then, not waiting for an answer, or explaining what "that" is, she adds, "Just be discreet."

And so we stayed at my parents' house that night, and slept together on a foldout couch in their basement. I was left to make up my own interpretation of what "discreet" meant to my mom. Did she mean we weren't to have wild sex and hang from the (nonexistent) chandeliers? (There was very little fear of *that* happening in my parents' home.) Or did she mean (maybe) that we should be sure that the ten-year-old foster child they had staying with them at the time remained innocently unaware of the fact that we were sleeping together, unmarried? I wasn't sure.

The point is that when my mother's strict ethical/moral rules came head-to-head with her love for her daughter and her desire for us to be close, and to spend time together, the love won.

* * *

I wasn't the kind of granddaughter my mother had been either, as evidenced in letters between her and her grandmother.

AUGUST 15, 1936 LETTER FROM MY MOTHER (AGE 10) TO HER GRANDMOTHER, NELLIE SANBORN

Dear Grandma,

I haven't answered your letter well at all. I had a good time at Aunt Grayces but I believe I had more fun with you. I sure hope you can come up this fall like you did last year.

It has been very hot here today. It was 104 this afternoon and tonight we are getting rain. It sure is raining here, and the wind is blowing.

I don't know if I told you about our little bantams. We have a hen and a rooster and the first time this summer she set she got six and raised 3. And today the second time she brought out 7 out of 8 eggs.

We had a little kitten that had sore eyes and didn't grow very well. Mother said it reminded her of the one Uncle Paul had when he lived with Mom and Dad. But it died today, it was David's we all felt very sorry. It was such a playful little thing.

Momma's having fried chicken for supper. We have just killed three so far. They aren't very big. The boys have all got their swimming suits on and are playing out in the rain.

We have had about three weeks of sweet corn. The cows cleaned it up quite well. We're having to herd cows and Lewis and David got poison ivy and I've got a little too.

Momma and Daddy went to Goodhue this afternoon and we kids and Grandpa stayed home. They went to sell their grain. We are planning on having an auction in the fall and selling some of our young stock...

Momma said I have wrote so much there won't be anything for her to say. Say hello to the rest of the folks from us.

From your loving granddaughter, Carol Powers

PS Please answer my letter. I like to get letters.

In 1939 my mother, now thirteen, reported in her journal that her grandfather had died, and that she and her fifteen-year-old brother Lewey stayed home to "keep things going" on the farm while their parents and two younger brothers went to Iowa for the funeral, a trip which would have lasted at least a couple of days. My mother and Lewey were left alone and charged with looking after the animals on the farm. "I kept care of the turkeys," she wrote. "We got 500. We got them the day Grandpa died. I also got the meals, got the cows, and many petty duties. Lewis cultivated and did the chores."

My goodness, I thought, reading this. To be solely responsible for 500 newly-arrived turkeys at the age of thirteen! ("Are you sure she didn't mean 50?" my husband says, when I tell him this. "She said 500…" I say, shaking my head.) Not an easy life on the farm…

Apparently they also had to deal with a pig who had gotten her head stuck in a can while the grownups were gone, as alluded to in this letter to my mother from her grandmother.

June 4, 1939 Letter from Nellie Sanborn to my mother (now 13)

My dear Carol,

It was very nice of you to write me that the folks got home, and how you got along with the turkeys. The old pig was not very considerate or she would have waited till the Boss got home before she put her head in the can.…I have my house full of flowers three big bouquets of peonies and they are very beautiful. The white ones are so large this year…And the roses are in bloom too. It tires me to go out to get them. But will do it. When I cannot pick flowers, might as well give up as no-count…I will write several other letters to take up the time…You write a nice letter Carol. Do it again. Love to everyone.

Grandma Sanborn

The letters between my great-grandmother and my grandmother, and between my mother and grandmother were likewise affectionate.

MAY 30, 1944 LETTER FROM NELLIE SANBORN TO HER DAUGHTER (MY GRANDMOTHER), WHO IS NOW 52 YEARS OLD.

Dear Effie,

I believe you have a birthday soon. But can't believe it is so long as it figures up since you was first in my arms. And old Dr. Reed said don't cry because it is a girl—our baby here is enough. How well I remember what he said. But never since have you been a disappointment and that all turned out all right.

Love, Mother

LETTER FROM MY GRANDMOTHER TO MY MOTHER (UNDATED, BUT PROBABLY AROUND 1947). WRITTEN FROM CRESCO, IOWA, WHERE MY GRANDMOTHER WAS VISITING HER MOTHER.

Dear Carol,

I wonder if you have any idea what your letter did for me. I love you so and you are everything I could wish for in a daughter. And I am so glad you are having fun with boyfriends. I didn't say anything about M. because I didn't know what to say. After all I have never seen him, he is just a shadowy guy that likes you, he shows his good sense there, and is confused about religion which shows he is a serious guy, didn't have too good a home life which is too bad. But you said you weren't in love with him so I didn't think about him so very much. I don't think Bert's lack of height is very important but maybe the other things are. What would happen if Bert were coming and W. asked you for a date? That might happen sometime. Wouldn't it be nice if you could roll the good qualities of each one all into one guy?

You have just as many friends as I have but mine were more bunched up than yours…you have lots of friends. Hartland is to you what Bonair is to me, and there is no one there I ever see. There is one girl I know there who has moved to town lately. I think I will call her tomorrow.

Mother thinks it is lonesome here…But someone has run in every day, and I am here. I wonder what she would think of my set-up, contemplating living alone during the week on a farm where no one would run in but maybe the neighbor children from across the road. Mother has many faults and I think I will try to avoid the mistakes she has made but I will probably make some worse ones.

There is an old lady next door who is past 80 and she cooks for her two bachelor sons and her invalid husband, and I think there is a young girl there too… and this dear sweet old lady is keeping house for the bunch…

Don't think because I have written a long letter that I am home-sick, but there isn't much to do here. Mother has gone to bed and it was too early for me to go to sleep so I wrote a letter.

Love from Mother

Plowing my way through all these old letters I realize that I seem to have broken a three-generation chain of mother/daughter love and mutual admiration. I wasn't part of this chain in my mom's family. I never had a feeling of complete acceptance and approval by either my mom or my grandmother, and I didn't have the admiration for them that my mother had had for her mother and grandmother.

Was it necessary for me to break the chain of daughterly admiration in my mother's family in order to complete that other chain? That chain of a love of reading and writing so strong that it was able to propel me out of a world in which an essential part of me couldn't thrive? I don't know why it would have been; and yet, it does seem that some kind of fierce resistance may have been necessary.

> *I'm twelve years old, passing through the kitchen. My mother is hosting a "coffee party" for a few friends in the next room. They are talking about nudity in films. "I don't think it will last," my mom says. "The human body is not beautiful." "She's wrong about that," I think, instantly, reflexively, automatically.*

The irony is that it was *her* interest in the arts that was the reason our bookshelves included a number of art books that would have provided me with a strong counterargument to what she had said about the human body, and had given me already at the age of twelve a broader perspective than the one she had.

But she was in so many ways the victim of a Puritanical upbringing: it often caused her, I believe, to compromise the person she might have been had she not been so shackled.

* * *

It is easy to see from these letters how much strength my mother and grandmother were able to draw from confiding in each other. My mother certainly wasn't able to get this kind of strength from me, and much of the strength she gave me I didn't appreciate, or even recognize, until after she was gone. Given both my own individual nature and the nature of the generation gap in the late 1960s and early 1970s, not only could my mother not draw strength from me; I was a source of considerable worry for her.

I'm about twenty-one. I come home late one night after a date with a divorced man I have recently met. He's an "older man" though not really all that old, probably just a few years older than me. I've just lost my virginity with him, and it was an underwhelming experience. But my mother knows, intuits. She's worried about me seeing this older man, this divorced man. "Are you still a virgin?" she asks me as I come in the door, a worried look on her face, almost tearful. "Yes, Mom!" I lie. A couple of years earlier she had asked me if I smoked marijuana, fearing, I am sure, to hear the answer. "Mom, don't ask me questions that you can't accept any answer to," I said. Good advice, I suppose, but the answer was cruel nonetheless. She was only doing her job, trying to bridge an essentially unbridgeable gap.

It makes me sad to realize how far short our relationship fell of what she would have liked it to be; and the only comfort I can give myself is knowing how strong and kind she was. Strong enough to overcome the hurt she must have felt at times—in fact often—because of the way I treated her. Strong enough to withstand the disappointment of never having been able to have the kind of close relationship with me that she had had with her mother. Kind enough to let me know that she could, and did, forgive me for it, even without saying so.

Fortunately, she probably didn't need to draw strength from me as much as her mother had needed to draw strength from her. I think she got a kind of support from my father that my grandmother didn't get from my grandfather. Also, my mother had gotten herself into a much bigger world than her mother ever had, by leaving the farm behind, by going to the university. I think that was very important to her.

During their courtship my mom often told my dad about things she was reading for her classes. "I only have 300 pages of *War and Peace* left. I passed page 1,000 last night. What a book! So good but so long winded..." she wrote in one letter. After alluding to the Achilles/tortoise metaphor, she concludes. "On that I close. Ask me no questions, I merely quote." It would have made sense for her to have shared this particular part of that 1300-page book in a letter to my father: as an engineering student, he might have been able to understand the metaphor, which requires a fairly sophisticated grasp of mathematics. Like my mother, I tried, and could not follow it at all.

In the postscript to another letter to him, she mentions her disgust with Thomas Paine. "Don't read T. Paine's Age of Reason," she wrote. "He takes each book of the Bible and debunks it. How I wish I could wring his neck."

I have no way of knowing for sure, but from what I've been able to gather about the relationship of my grandparents, I think it is fairly unlikely that this kind of intellectual dialogue is something they engaged in. The evidence suggests otherwise.

For example, in a diary entry in 1966, when she was in her seventies, my grandmother wrote "Elmer went to town so I was able to watch what I wanted on TV." (What my grandfather liked to watch on TV was "professional" wrestling.) And in a letter to my mom the following year she wrote, "I am sorry I said the TV programs were for morons. That same day in the evening was the NY Philharmonic Orchestra, and Leonard Bernstein is definitely not a moron! What a flow of words. I tried but couldn't keep up with him, and then the beautiful music..."

* * *

Though it was not a source of our arguments—we argued about other things, usually limitations on some aspect of my freedom—my mother had remarked from an early age, not infrequently, that I had been "born into the wrong class." One of the things I hated the most was when I would ask for something and she would say, "That's not necessary." (After all, most of the things I wanted were not really necessary.)

I'm in graduate school, reading King Lear. When Goneril and Regan start taking away all of Lear's privileges—in particular his knights—and he protests, they answer by telling him he doesn't need them. "O, reason not the need!" he cries out, in agony, and adds an impassioned, outraged cry from the heart. "Allow not nature more than nature needs/Man's life's as cheap as beast's..."

*"**That** is what I should have said to my mother," I think.*

One thing is certain: unlike my mom, I never wanted to be anything like my mother, and until after she died I resisted seeing that in many ways I *was* like her: sometimes for the better, sometimes for the worse.

To My Mom on Mother's Day (1989)

Analysis of the 10 Most Important Things I Learned from My Mother:

1. *"If you can't say something nice, don't say anything at all." This is good advice, though it must be used with some discretion. If, for example, we were to follow this rule to the letter, it would have been impossible to discuss the events in Washington for the entire decade of the 1980s! On balance, however, this is a good rule. What really underlies it is the impulse to be kind.*

2. *"There will always be some who have more than you, and some who have less." I have found this to be absolutely true, and absolutely helpful. Knowing this stifles envy and greed, and promotes gratitude for one's blessings in life.*

3. *"You only have to do it this once, and then if you don't like it you don't have to do it again." Words I hated to hear, but the lesson learned, a valuable one. Keep an open mind. Explore. Experiment. Overcome your prejudices.*

4. *"Always vote." You never said this, you just always did it. After a certain period, you even always voted correctly! No problem with this lesson. I'm not as faithful a voter as you, but I'm better than 95% of my countrymen, and trying to improve.*

5. *"Make your bed." No contest. But what do you do when your husband gets out of bed after you, and he doesn't make it?*

6. *"Never let the sun set on your anger." You extended this rule to "Never leave home angry." Sometimes hard to do, but good advice. It taught me forgiveness, and more importantly taught me that you can love someone and be furious with them simultaneously.*

7. *"You should have been born into a different class." Maybe true, maybe not. In any case, this encouraged me to set my sights high, so I could overcome the injustice visited upon me by birth in the lowly class I found myself in!*

8. *Learn about your cultural heritage, and your family history, and treasure them. Keep your own history alive. You never put this into words, exactly, either. This too I learned by your example. I think it's great that when you married a Swede, you tried to learn Swedish. (Failure to actually learn it is beside the point.) I think it's great that you wanted to name me Brita, even though I'm glad you didn't because you wouldn't have been the only one unable to pronounce it correctly!*

   It is the impulse to explore, the relish you took in passing on to us stories about you and your brothers that taught me from a very early age that narrative springs from human experience everywhere, not just in books, not just in stories about famous people. The stories you told me about "horse mittens" and "dog teeth," Napoleon the goose, and "Carol Busybus Powers" were my favorites.

9. *There are many things in life more important than having lots of money. Almost everything in fact. Once again, by example. Once again, priceless. (No pun intended.) Once again, no contest.*

10. *"That's not necessary." Well, okay, Mom. Nine out of ten isn't bad, is it?*

Love, Janet

I'm so glad I said these things to her when I did. For as it turned out, we weren't going to have much more time together.

There's another very important thing she taught me that I didn't think to include on that list, probably because it hadn't yet fully sunk in just how important that lesson was going to be for me in my life.

*I'm about seven, I think—first or second grade. I come home from school one day and as soon as I get into the house I throw myself into my mother's lap. "Susie said my dress was ugly!" I say, bursting into tears. She lets me cry for a bit, stroking my back in a comforting way. Then, when the sobbing has subsided, she asks, gently, "Do **you** think your dress is ugly?" The answer is simple, and clear. "No!" I say, lifting my head, and sitting up straight. I knew it was a pretty dress!*

There are so many things my mother could have said in response to that crushing hurt. But she chose the one that was absolutely the best. In the simplest way possible, she let me know that I should trust my own judgment, and believe in myself.

And she let me figure out that important truth on my own, without overtly telling me.

Without making me think it was *her* idea.

My mother at our wedding, 1985

Too Soon Gone

In 1983, when she was fifty-seven, my mother was diagnosed with multiple myeloma, a bone marrow cancer. She was told that most people with the disease died within a couple of years after diagnosis, and at first it seemed she would accept this prognosis, as the dutiful nurse she was. Who was she to argue with doctors?

I don't remember the phone call in which I received this news. But I do remember thinking that her position *vis* à *vis* the disease was entirely too passive, and that I had to get home as soon as I could to see if I could rouse her into a state of greater resistance. I was both working and studying at Hunter College, but my spring break was not far away. I waited however long it was—ten days?—and then took the train home, determined to use the thirty-six hours of train travel from New York to St. Paul to pull my thoughts and emotions together, and plan my campaign to keep my mother alive.

It worked, kind of. I roared into town, a whirlwind of positive energy, full of suggestions for alternative cures, medical facilities, treatments. I knew my cyclone approach was a bit overbearing, but I also knew I had to work fast. I wasn't able to stay home for very long, and I felt I had to make significant progress while I was there. So I pushed my ideas aggressively, playing the clown to make the aggression more bearable, trying to make her laugh, trying to cheer her up. My mother had always been so relentlessly optimistic. I had never seen her in such a defeated, negative frame of mind. It was a terrible thing to see.

She was enthusiastic about none of my ideas, and she had a particularly strong negative reaction to my suggestion that there was an alternative healing center in Tijuana that we should look into. "We can't do *that*," she said, giving me a pitiful look of helpless entreaty. I had pretty much known she was going to reject the idea of seeking medical treatment in Mexico, so I was all prepared with a local alternative. There was a doctor in St. Louis Park, a suburb across town, who was doing very interesting work with megavitamin therapy, I told her. "St. Louis *Park?!*" she objected. ("But we have perfectly good doctors right here in Coon Rapids," was the implication.) "Mom: it's either that or Tijuana," I insisted, mercilessly. "Well, okay," she agreed, and off we drove across town, to meet Dr. Shemesh.

Dr. Shemesh was a wonderful doctor, with a very sympathetic bedside manner. He explained that what he had been doing with his patients was basically providing them with nutritional reinforcement, to help strengthen them against the damages wrought by chemotherapy. He was gentle and kind, and he didn't push too hard. When the bill for the high-quality vitamins he was recommending for my mother came to more than $100 and she hardly even blinked before writing the check, I knew she was ready to fight. When she gave me a wan smile, and said, "I guess we could try it," I felt a warm rush of affection for her. I knew how hard it was for her to spend money like that. She had never been able to get over the effects of growing up poor during the Depression.

We went to the grocery store together to get some of the foods Dr. Shemesh had recommended. And while we were there I tried to retrain her in her fruit and vegetable buying habits. The Depression years mentality had never left her. She always went for produce that was nearly spoiled already (the produce that was on sale). "It's cheap because it's no good, Mom. Don't get the rotten stuff. Only the best is good enough, that's your new slogan." Again that helpless, wan look came back. Poor Mom! This was so hard for her.

The other tactic I had come up with, after reading Dr. Bernie Siegel's book *Love, Medicine, and Miracles,* was to get her to laugh, to unleash that healing power he had spoken of. "You gotta laugh, Mom, it's good for you," I said. She had an offbeat sense of humor; often the things she laughed at the hardest were things hardly anyone else found funny, but so what? We talked about her favorite funny stories, films she could watch with my dad, to get those endorphins working.

Meanwhile I hammed it up with my "Only the best is good enough" routine, *ad nauseum* to the point where that too became funny. Just before leaving the house to return to New York I put post-it notes on the refrigerator, inside the cupboards, in her purse, on her dresser. "Only the best is good enough," "Remember: only the best is good enough!" and "Don't forget, now: only the best is good enough," hoping that when I was gone and quiet had once again descended on their home, these too would make her laugh, or at least smile.

My plan worked for a while: my mother decided she didn't want to die within a year or two, and that if there was anything she could do about it, she wasn't going to. She took to her health food routine with, if not enthusiasm, at least honest and dutiful compliance. And she began to collect funny anecdotes from *Reader's Digest* to put in her purse, so they would be right at hand, and she wouldn't forget to laugh.

The plan—a combination of chemotherapy, radiation, vitamins, and laughter—worked for seven years. And in those seven years, she was able to dance at our wedding; go to China with my dad; come to my husband's first one-man show in Soho; and continue to work—up until the cancer came calling again, and this time wouldn't go away.

Multiple myeloma does win in the end: it's only a matter of time. Triumph over the disease is found by living your life as fully and as well as you can before it makes its final demands. In that sense, my mother *did* beat the disease. She won.

And then it was time for the end. It came in the autumn of 1990, seven years after her diagnosis, though the signs were clear by late summer that the time was drawing near. At a family gathering in Wisconsin one day, she moved her leg the wrong way and ignited an excruciating pain that never went away after that.

Anyone who has ever been in the position of living far away from a close member of their family who is dying knows the difficult choices that must be made. How do you properly gauge "the right time" to be there? How do you keep your life going, more or less, and how do you know when to put your life on hold? It isn't easy.

I was lucky. I had understanding employers who allowed me to go home for a week in September when the first part of her final descent began. That was an important time for me and my mother. It was the last "normal" time we had together, the last time we were able to talk with each other. It was during this time that she asked me to be the one to make whatever end-of-life medical decisions would need to be made. "Shouldn't it be Dad?" I asked. "He can't do it," she said. "It has to be you."

During that visit we had the luxury of time spent together talking, reading, just being together. "Wonderful Janet!" she said one day when I walked into her room at the nursing home. "And to think I didn't want you to come," she added. This was also the visit when she remarked, "I never knew what a nice person you are," which by that time I was able to take in the spirit in which it was offered—as her grateful realization that yes, I really had turned out well—rather than as a backhanded insult.

She died on October 25. I was able to be with her in the end because one of the nurses who was caring for her—who had been both a high school classmate of mine, and one of my mom's student nurses—called me in New York and let me know that her time was almost up. Breaking with protocol, she advised me not to wait until my next planned visit. "She's starting to say her goodbyes," she said tearfully, and that made me know I had to be on the next plane I could get on.

My husband came with me that time: and we got there a few days before she died. I remember seeing the page-a-day calendar at the nursing station as I went out for one of my rejuvenating walks around the neighborhood a day or two before she died. "Is this the day my mom will die?" I thought, and hard on that thought, "I don't know how to live without my mom."

But it turns out, I did know how. She had taught me so well!

Perhaps the most important thing of all was something that she had said to me on one of those days in my September visit. "It really doesn't matter, you know," she said. "I'll either be here—or there," gesturing with her finger, heavenward.

And that turned out, like so many of the things she had taught me in the time we had together, to be true. Though I missed her acutely in the first couple of years after she was gone, and have never really stopped missing her presence in the world, I have also never felt that the loss was total. She has always been "there" for me.

Changed, Changed Utterly

My mother died when I was thirty-seven years old–sadly (for her, for me, for them) before any of her grandchildren were born. Also sad, it really wasn't until after she died and I had to learn how to live my life without her that I realized how critical her continuing existence had been to my own.

One of the first ways this came home to me is that once she was gone, I found that it was impossible for me to continue to write the weekly letters I had always written home. This was a point of some agony, since I knew how much my father loved reading them, and that surely now he needed them more than ever before. But I couldn't help what I couldn't help. And once my mother was gone, I discovered to my surprise and dismay that among other things, she had apparently always been the audience I was writing for. It was her sensibility above all that had formed mine, and her sensibility to which I was eagerly returning, with my observations of the world that was still opening up to me.

Another thing that happened is that almost from the moment of her death, I realized that it was as if suddenly I was seeing for the first time a photograph of her, rich in nuance, beautifully complex, with all the infinitely subtle shades of gray: and that all my life prior to that I had been judging her on the basis of my squinty-eyed view of a negative. Her shortcomings did not disappear, but they did recede into the background, taking their proper place in the larger scheme of things, and her true nature–her strength, intelligence, generosity, and wisdom–became clear to me in a way that they never had been before, when my attention was fixed on her myriad, though minor, imperfections.

I had always felt guilty about my impatience with her, and sometimes my feeling ashamed of her. I knew what a good person she was, and what a good mother. How could I be so impatient, so ungrateful? And yet often I couldn't help it. She would say the most embarrassing things! Like the time I took her and my dad to a Chinese restaurant in Minneapolis, and she kept accidentally calling the chopsticks "pork chops." She also pronounced the word "wash" as "warsh," and "language" as "langridge." (She often said, ironically enough, that profanity showed "poverty of langridge.") I don't know where these pronunciations came from, probably from her mother? I looked it up when I was working on this book and learned that these pronunciations belong to a dialect called "Midlands" American English, and that it is Scotch/Irish in origin. So it may have come down from some part of our family tree that started in the British Isles. Or maybe it came from Iowa?

Anyway, these things embarrassed me, and I was ashamed of myself for being embarrassed by my mother.

One year she was invited to help write the national board exams for practical nurses. When she returned from New York City, where the meeting had been held, and was telling me and my New Yorker boyfriend about the trip, one of the things she mentioned was her astonishment at the size of "those enormous granaries" she had seen as they flew in over Manhattan. Fortunately my boyfriend didn't say anything at the time, but later he said to me, "Do you realize she was talking about the **World Trade Center**?!" and added, "Do you have any idea how much grain could be held in those buildings?!!" He laughed, not unkindly; and of course he had spared her feelings at the time of her telling her story, and not said anything, just nodded.

But I couldn't laugh, not at all, and when I told my best friend about this, she hadn't laughed either, and had understood right away. "Oh, that's so sad," she said, and when my boyfriend asked why, she said, "Because of the gulf..."

Gradually, through the years, I realized that a good deal of the tension in our relationship had been rooted in my fierce struggle not to be like her: gradually I realized how much I *was* like her in many ways, for both better and worse, and that on balance this was not such a bad thing.

My mother was not perfect, and she did not suddenly become perfect in my eyes when she was gone. But almost as soon as she was gone, I could at least begin to see her more clearly. At least I could see how hard she had tried to do the best she could; and just how good that was.

Me and my mom, 1953

JANET JOY HULSTRAND
(1953-

"CARPE DIEM—SEIZE THE DAY!"

My Mother, My First Editor

One of those things that I do not myself remember, but remember being told about, happened when I was about three years old. The story goes that I was in a grocery store with my mother and there was a book I wanted. She told me no, I could not have the book, and, enraged, I threw one of those tantrums that makes everyone in the vicinity cringe and want nothing more than to get as far away from the scene as possible, as quickly as possible.

So, from the beginning my mother's role in my literary life was an ambiguous one. On the one hand she would do something as capriciously cruel as deny me the acquisition of a new book I wanted. On the other hand, the bedtime stories she told me; the narrative lullabies she sang to me—the same ones that had been sung to her by her mother and for all I know by my grandmother's mother before that—the regular trips to the library; and her somewhat uncharacteristic indulging of my bedtime pleas to "just let me finish this chapter," were all ways that she instilled and encouraged in me a love of reading.

She also encouraged me to write from an early age, and took clear pleasure in my first steps into the world of publication. "Janet had a letter from *Children's Playmate* magazine last week," she wrote in a letter to her parents in March, 1963, when I was nine. "She won a year's subscription for writing a piece on the pilgrims last November. She was quite thrilled but wished it could be converted to cash."

In the same month, in a notebook she had dedicated to reporting on my progress after I had grown past the pages of my baby book, she wrote, "She's a budding author. Has written one story about the

Revolutionary War, one about the Civil War, and is now working on some mysteries."

She didn't mention her key editorial role in those budding efforts, nor did she appear to realize that the reason I had abandoned the "historical novels" I had started had anything to do with her. But I remember distinctly that when she had read the draft pages of those first efforts, she had suggested to me that maybe I should "write about something you know, something about your own life." I thought that was the dumbest thing I had ever heard.

What I didn't know was that the reason for her comment surely had to do with the fact that I had opened the story about a little girl in Gettysburg by stating that she had awakened to the sound of cannon fire, a sound she had heard every morning for far longer than the battle had lasted. Nor did I understand why my mother had suggested that the mother of the young heroine in my Revolutionary War story probably would not have become pregnant while her husband was away at war, explaining that "babies need fathers." "The baby HAS a father," I replied, with impatient disdain. "He's just not there right now."

Hampered as she was by her reticence to discuss the details of human reproduction with a nine-year-old, she was stuck giving me not very helpful editorial advice. I'd like to say that if she had pointed out the need for engaging in research when writing about a historical period it might have opened up a whole new career path for me. But the truth is that I probably would not have listened to that either, bent as I was on forging my own path in life and convinced, like so many pre-adolescent girls, that my mother really didn't know very much.

In any case, I didn't feel like my life thus far had given me much to write about. I was going to need to "go somewhere" too, in order for that to happen.

From St. Paul to Cincinnati

Janet & Darlene taken to Berto

On N. Simpson Street, with my cousin Darlene

My "journey" began in St. Paul, Minnesota, where I lived for the first few years of my life, in a brand-new house my parents had bought in a tract housing development in a suburb called Roseville.

Like most people, my memories from those early years are an odd assortment of random events.

*I'm three years old, and to amuse my baby brother who is getting his hair cut (or something), I stick a peanut up my nose to make him laugh. I do it several times and several times snort it out, to his giggles and hand-clapping delight. Then I push it up **even further** (to amuse him **even more**) and it won't come out.*

* * *

I'm probably about four: I've drawn a spider web with my crayons, and it's perfect! Because that one drawing has turned out so well, I draw a great many more spider webs that day. (This is the last time I remember feeling pleased with my drawing skills.)

* * *

I wake up (kind of) from a nap and go outside to look for my mom. The next thing I know I am lying on the couch covered with sandburs while she picks them out of my clothing.

* * *

For some reason a few of us kids have decided to see how many of us can fit into a doghouse and I am crammed uncomfortably into the back corner. (Does this suggest that this great idea was mine?)

* * *

My friend Billy and I are chasing each other around the circle of rooms in their house across the street from our house. As I run through the kitchen past his mom, who is making liverwurst sandwiches, she gently pulls my thumb out of my mouth and generously coats it with liverwurst. (She knows I hate liverwurst.) She looks at me inquiringly, I frown—then shrug, and wipe the

*liverwurst off on my pants. She smiles, shakes her head, and Billy
and I happily continue the chase.*

When I was five we moved to Cincinnati. My father was involved
in aerospace projects, and his new job was working for Avco, on a
pre-Apollo mission. It was a big, bold move for my parents: they
were not in Minnesota anymore, not even anywhere in the upper
Midwest: to all our relatives, this was a move "out East."

SCHOOL DAYS 1959-60
COLERAIN

We moved in the middle of the year, so I had to change schools for kindergarten. I don't remember it as being particularly traumatic. My dad was the one to take me to my first day of school in the new kindergarten, and he reported that when he brought me to my classroom I strode right in and "didn't even look back." I do remember that in that kindergarten I got an "unsatisfactory" grade in scissors skills. (But honestly, they had us cutting fabric with those blunt, rounded paper scissors: what did they expect?!)

We lived for the first few months in a rented house in a neighborhood called College Hill. Then my parents bought a brand-new Cape Cod style red brick house in a new suburban development in Colerain Township. It was in fact a *very* new development; only a few houses had been carved out of the woods when we moved there, and this fact provided me and my friends with many hours of happy playing in the woods, by the creek, hours that filled my imagination with stories about pioneers and Indians, and led me to my passion for reading books about them—or was it the books that led to all the fort-building and Indian village construction we engaged in? I'm not sure which came first, but both were really satisfying.

Those were my two favorite activities as a child: playing in the woods, and reading. I was always an early riser; in the summertime I would get up almost as soon as it was light and go outside, and would come inside only to eat, use the bathroom, or read. I remember one of many battles with my mom was whether or not I could stay up one night, to watch the *Dick Van Dyke* show, which began at 9:30 pm. She said I could watch if I would promise to stay in bed the next morning until 8 am, which I felt was incredibly unreasonable. I refused, and while the family watched the show that night I lay on the floor with my head at the top of the stairs and listened.

That neighborhood was a wonderful place to be a child. We had best friends next door: Bruce, David, and Mary Houghton, and a little bit later their brother Johnny was born. My best friend was Mary, who was a couple of years younger than me. Occasionally we would have a falling out, but most of the time she was my best companion.

There was also a girl named Charlotte. Charlotte was one of two "only children" in the neighborhood. In those days an "only child" was often assumed to be almost automatically a spoiled child, and Charlotte filled the bill. (The other "only child" in the neighborhood fit the stereotype of having everything she wanted; I remember my awe when she opened her closet door one day and I saw the wealth of new toys and games within. But she was a nice girl, and fun to play with; she was not really spoiled at all.)

Charlotte was another matter. She must have had a very domineering personality because one day something peculiar occurred in my first-grade class. My teacher called me up to her desk and asked me, not unkindly, but very curiously, "Janet, why have you written Charlotte's name on your paper?"

Our assignment had been to draw a picture of children, and to print the word "children." Apparently Charlotte's aggressive coaching of me in the spelling of her name had interfered in my brain to the point that when I start spelling a word with "Ch" that is where it inevitably led. "I don't know..." I said to my teacher, honestly, just as perplexed as she was.

A few years later—we were probably about eight or nine—I went to Charlotte's house to play one day, and before we got a chance to play she gave me an arch look, paused, and then said, as she counted out her advantages on her fingers. "Let's see: what do I have that you don't have? I have my own phonograph; I have my own portable TV; and I have my very own Princess telephone." Then she looked at me as if waiting for a response. I don't think I said anything. What was there to say? I do remember that my main reaction was a kind of perplexed boredom.

There is one other incident I remember about Charlotte. Again, I don't remember how old I was at the time: but at least nine, I would think. It might have been when my mom was in the hospital after the birth of my baby sister. I was playing at Charlotte's house and was supposed to stay there until my dad came to pick me up. But Charlotte was being so unpleasant about whatever the board game was that we were playing, that I said, "I'm going home now." "You can't!" she said, triumphantly, and of course once so challenged, I had to. "I can too," I said. "I'll go to Jenny's house." It was wintertime and I remember her mom helping me on with my coat, and the worried look on her face. Thinking back on it, I'm very surprised that she let me go alone. She shouldn't have! I had to walk through the woods, and climb over a very large fallen tree trunk, in the dark, then cross a street and go around the corner to get to Jenny's house.

Once I got there I was too shy, or embarrassed, to knock on the door so I stood out on the car port thinking about what I should do next. Fortunately, soon enough the door opened (I suppose Charlotte's mother had called there to make sure I got there safely), and Jenny's mom looked out. "Janet?" she said. "Are you out there?" She invited me to come inside, and kindly asked me no questions.

After we had moved back to Minnesota, I heard very little from Charlotte, but once in a while she would write to let me know what she had that I didn't have. (A red Mustang and a nineteen-year-old boyfriend "going on 20" one letter, written when we were sixteen, informed me.)

Then it was years and years before I heard from her again, and when I did it was through a Facebook friend invite. I accepted her invitation but it wasn't long before she had unfriended me. Her path had led her into some kind of fundamentalist Christianity, and mine had not. She probably didn't approve of my politics.

Anyway, even back then it had been better, most of the time, to play with Mary.

But there was also a lot of time devoted to reading. My mother would take me to the library once a week, and her instructions were that I had to bring enough books home to last me a week: that was usually a pretty tall stack. I loved reading the books in the

Childhood of Famous American Series; the biography of Julia Ward Howe was my favorite one. In general I preferred to read about writers rather than nurses (like Clara Barton) or seamstresses (like Betsy Ross). I also loved reading about Native Americans. One of my favorite books was *Indian Captive* by Lois Lenski, which was based on the true story of Mary Jemison, who had been adopted by a Seneca family after the rest of her family was killed by the Shawnee in an attack on a pioneer settlement. She grew up with the Seneca, and when she was given the opportunity to return to life among English-speaking settlers she chose instead to remain with the Seneca. I also loved *Caddie Woodlawn*, much more than the Little House series of books. The Little House books were okay: the details about frontier life—making candles, building log homes, etc.—were interesting to me, but the characters seemed too saccharine, too true to "type." They didn't really interest me, and I didn't really believe in them. Caddie was always getting into trouble for doing things that weren't really bad, they were just "unladylike," and she had no shame about anything she was doing. She was much more interesting and fun than Laura.

I can remember sitting in one of our comfortable armchairs inside on a summer day, devouring one book or another, hearing a knock on the door and someone saying "Can Janet come out?" "She's reading," my mother would say, as if that answered the question completely.

And yet, I did spend a great deal of time outdoors. It was so much fun to play in the woods there in that new "subdivision" just being freshly carved out of a wilderness that had in fact not *that* long ago still belonged to Native Americans. I loved to think about who had been there earlier, in those very woods, as we played. There was a creek and the creek had huge trees on either side, some of them with vines thick and strong enough for us to swing on, and (of course) we would make Tarzan calls as we did so. Often we would play all day long in the woods, and we became very engaged in building "Indian" and pioneer villages in the wooded back section of our yard where some very large beech trees had been taken down. The tree trunks stayed there for a while, and we were able to make quite an impressive rustic "kitchen counter" with one of them. I took great pleasure in naming all of the younger children pioneer names (Lucretia, Jedediah), or "Indian" names ("Blue Jay," I remember, is the name I gave to Johnny Houghton.)

There was also a pond right next door to the Houghtons, on the other side of their house. It was not actually a pond, it was a basement that had been dug for a house that was never built, and which eventually filled up with rain. After one big storm, a tree that had fallen into the pond provided us with a great way to venture out toward the middle of it. This was something we had of course been forbidden to do, because it was dangerous. But we did it anyway, and one day Mary managed to get all of her hair wet when she nearly fell backward into the pond from her perch on that tree. She pulled herself up and away from the water looking a bit like Medusa.

When, more than fifty years later, it occurred to me to look up images of our old address on Google, it was a very unsettling discovery to find that both the Houghtons' house and ours had been razed, the basements filled in, the yards left in an unkempt tangle. My overly dramatic imagination leapt instantly to questions about why fifty-year-old brick homes with full, solid, concrete basements had been torn down. Was there a toxic leak there? Is that what had killed my mother and my brother before their time? (She at the age of sixty-four, he at the age of fifty-seven?)

But a little (just a little!) more research revealed the reason: there is a big Kroger's grocery store, and a MoneyGram now, right next to where we lived for five happy years; and our yard had become literally part of the parking lot.

The forest is no longer a forest, and the creek has no doubt long since been covered over.

They paved paradise, put up a parking lot, indeed.

Being Swedish-American

My mom was in charge of my cultural education—in addition to her love of reading, and her encouraging of my writing, she shared with her children her love of music, first and foremost Broadway musicals, and also theater. She took me to a stage production of *The Miracle Worker* while we still lived in Cincinnati; and also to a road show production of the Broadway musical *Camelot*, both very memorable experiences. She also pressured me to try church choir as an eight-year-old, something I resisted vigorously. "You're forcing me!" I objected, scowling, and she agreed that she was. "But I'll only force you this once," she said. "I think you'll actually like it. And if you don't, you don't have to go again." When she asked me after my first practice how it was, and I replied, sullenly, "Okay I guess," she was smart enough not to insist on claiming victory. She knew that if she had I would have been forced to forgo choir, and I didn't want to do that.

Because she was right. I *did* like it. I liked the singing, and we also got to wear robes of a rich, shiny, iridescent blue, with a shiny white satin V-shaped stole.

Later, as an adult, I teasingly asked her why she hadn't forced me to go out for the school plays in high school, since one of my few regrets in life is that I hadn't done that.

Sometimes moms just can't win.

But it was my dad who was in charge of my political education. He came from a family of strong DFLers: Minnesota's Democratic Farmer-Labor party, the party of Hubert Humphrey and Walter Mondale. My mom's family was that bewildering variety of Republicans of whom it was hard to understand *why* their allegiance was on the side of the bankers and successful businessmen of this world. I guess some of it must have had to do with a resentment born during those Depression years when, as my mom later remembered (and told me) the kids on welfare had gotten the good fruit, while she and her brothers were stuck eating the half-rotten fruit no one wanted to buy. (They should have accepted welfare, unashamedly. They worked hard, and they were poor: they needed help!) But they had a stubborn pride about not accepting "charity" along with (I guess) disdain for those who did.

Anyway. There may have been other reasons too. But for whatever reason, my mom's side of the family was not Democratic.

My dad started working on converting my mom politically during their courtship, but she had continued to vote Republican for the first years of their marriage. But by 1960, when I was seven years old and John F. Kennedy was running for president against Richard Nixon, my dad saw that he had a potential ally in me, and he used it to full advantage. One day he came home with a gift for me, a black felt skirt with a donkey on it (with those little plastic eyes that rolled). My mom made a remark that seemed both superfluous and very odd to me. "Why didn't you get her an elephant?" she said, and he just laughed.

Shortly afterward, one night he whispered in my ear. "Go and ask your mom if it's really true that she's planning to vote for Tricky Dick..." I did as he suggested and when I did, she chided him ("Bert!") in mock anger.

I think she probably did vote for "Tricky Dick" that year despite the mounting pressure from my dad, and now from me too, to do otherwise. (She was disdainful of Catholic beliefs and practices in general, and also concerned that a Catholic president would be prone to "take orders from the Pope.") But after that election, I think she gave up: she began to vote as a Democrat, and was pretty reliably on our side politically for the rest of her life. By the time Walter Mondale was running for president against Ronald Reagan in 1984, I was able to respond with full confidence that both of my parents were going to vote for him when asked by one of my husband's aunts. We were at her lake cabin in Minnesota, and she had been elbowed by my mother-in-law as she was about to go into a lengthy tirade against Mondale. "Janet's *for* Mondale, you know," his mom stage whispered to her sister, whose eyes widened as she looked at me inquiringly. "But your *parents* aren't, are they?..." she said. I smiled and nodded affirmatively; and that ended *that* conversation.

The other thing I got from my dad was being Swedish-American. He was 100 percent Swedish-American.

Between the years 1861 and 1881, approximately 150,000 Swedes immigrated into the United States. Although I don't know the details of my great-grandfather's departure from Sweden (from Småland, in the southern part of the country), it is likely that, like many of his compatriots, he left because of the increasingly difficult conditions for Swedish farmers. A growing population and crop failures during those years combined to make the "promised land" in the United States attractive enough for them to venture across an ocean and say goodbye to their homeland, knowing they would almost certainly never see their families again.

He came into the US sometime before the immigration station opened on Ellis Island in 1892, which means that he would have passed through the processing center at Castle Clinton, in lower Manhattan. That is where he would have changed his name, from Gustafson (a very common Swedish name) to Hultstrand, a fabricated, and fairly unusual name, which had the benefit of sounding (and being) very Swedish (a "hult" is a copse, a small group of trees; and "strand" is a beach). Sometime later the "t" was dropped from our name, making it even more unusual.

Did he change his name merely to have a more unique name, or was there some other reason? ("Well, why do people change their names?" Jack Kerouac asks, in *Satori in Paris*. "Have they done anything bad, are they ashamed of their real names?")

Since my great-grandfather had made no attempt to sound less Swedish with his name change, my guess is he just didn't want to be one among hundreds of other Gustafsons; and I must say it has been nice all my life not to be one of hundreds, and by now thousands, of Gustafsons.

I don't know how long he stayed in New York, but probably not very long: most of the Swedes entering the country were poor farmers, and they got out of the big city as quickly as they could, and headed west to where they could stake a claim to free land through the Homestead Act of 1862. And so, like many other Swedish farmers, he made his way to southeastern Minnesota, where in exchange for a small filing fee, he was given a plot of land to farm by the US government, with the stipulation that he had to continue farming it for at least five years. (The land was not really theirs to give away, of course; but that is another story.)

His plot was in Goodhue County, near the town of Cannon Falls, in a Swedish Lutheran parish called Spring Garden. The Spring Garden church is still there, and still active: a number of my ancestors, my grandparents, and one of my dad's brothers are buried there. When I went there with my husband one evening in the early 1980s and we were looking around the cemetery, a local woman asked where I came from and what I was doing there, in a friendly way. When she learned I was a Hulstrand she was full of questions, and greetings to pass on to my dad, my uncles. "I felt famous, like a Kennedy or something..." I said to my husband later that night.

Although my dad was born in Minnesota, and so were his parents, his first language was Swedish; like so many children in US history, he did not learn English until he started school. His first school was a one-room schoolhouse he walked a mile to with his brothers, and skied to when there was enough snow. I knew that their skis wouldn't have been fancy store-bought skis: my dad's family was too poor for that. But it was interesting, as one of the tidbits shared at the funeral eulogy given for my Uncle George many years later, to learn, from one of the neighbor "girls" (by then in her nineties) who had walked to school with my dad and his brothers, that their "skis" were in fact more precisely "old flat boards with leather straps." It is typical of my father not to have gone into too much detail, nor to have emphasized the humble nature of their skis. Thus I had retained a wonderfully romantic view of those winter mornings when they would ski to school across the snow.

The rural parish they grew up in was undilutedly Swedish-American. This is what Scandinavian immigration to Minnesota, in any case, was like. Swedes settled with (and married) other Swedes, Norwegians with Norwegians, Danes with Danes, Finns with Finns, and so on for at least a couple of generations. So the language spoken in my father's home, and in their church, was Swedish.

My dad was the one in his family to buck the trend and marry a woman who was not even Scandinavian. My mom's side of the family was a kind of Northern European hash—a little bit of this, a little bit of that (English, Irish (or Welsh?); Pennsylvania Dutch (which really is German, so why did my mom always say "Pennsylvania Dutch"?); and a tiny tiny bit of French (Huguenot, naturally, my family being Protestants all the way back).

Anyway. It was nice to be at least one half *something* that was very clear.

All of my cousins on the Hulstrand side of the family were also 100 percent Swedish-American, since their fathers (my dad's brothers) had done what any good Swedish-American boy should do: they had found themselves Swedish-American wives. One of my cousins was visiting me in New York when I was about thirty, and it somehow came out in conversation that my mom was not Swedish-American. There was a stunned pause, and then my cousin said, "Do you mean to tell me you're not 100 percent Swedish?"

People have often asked, when I tell this anecdote, whether this was a good thing or a bad thing in my cousin's mind. "It was neither good nor bad," I say. "It was simply unbelievable."

One of the things that was nicest about being Swedish-American was the way Christmas was celebrated. In Scandinavian homes in general, and certainly in my grandparents' home, Christmas Eve was the highlight of the celebration: Christmas Day was most definitely anticlimactic in comparison. And while we did not have the same traditions as my father and his brothers had had, riding off to a candlelit country church late at night in a horse-drawn carriage across snowy fields under a starry sky, there was plenty of special mystery and beauty to the fact that the celebration took place at night.

For the women, the hours before dinner were focused on cooking of course, while the men sat in the living room, smoking pipes and playing chess. I remember the Swedish meatballs my grandmother made (they were very good); and the *dopp i grytan*, a savory gravy for dipping bread in, which would simmer on the woodstove before the meal. I remember my grandmother inviting us to taste it, in her sing-song-y Swedish voice. There was also *lutefisk*, a Scandinavian "must" on Christmas Eve (it is codfish soaked in lye), which I managed to avoid ever even tasting until I was well into my twenties, because my older cousins made such a fuss about how awful it was. (And the smell was indeed vile!) My grandparents did not insist, did not even give any indication of disapproving of those of us who politely declined.

It's Christmas Eve and after the food has been served and eaten, the conversation among the adults goes on and on, in a kind of pleasant drone. We kids stay at the table until dessert has been served too. I don't mind staying there: I'm mesmerized by the little Swedish angel chimes placed in the middle of the table, with their little brass angels going round and round and round, propelled by the air currents generated by the candles. The brass pieces

*that hang from their little feet make the most lovely tinkling
sound as they hit the bells. And if you look up at the ceiling, there
is a fascinating pattern created by the turning of the fan that
moves the little angels round and round...*

Then, late at night there would be the opening of the presents
around the Christmas tree, and often, though not always, Santa
would appear with a sack of toys. I don't know who was under the
fake beard when I was a child, probably my grandfather, or maybe
one of my uncles: later it became my oldest cousin, George, and I
remember the year my little brother kept insisting that that was
Georgie under the beard, all the while quite clearly hoping that he
was wrong.

The most wonderful Christmastime tradition of all, however,
was one I didn't know about until I was grown up. That is, the Feast
of St. Lucia on December 13, which marks the beginning of
Christmas festivities in Sweden; and once I knew about it, I insti-
tuted it in our home also. I began the year we were married. I had
told my husband there would be "better things to come" once we
were married. He probably did not imagine that by that I meant I
would come into our bedroom before dawn one morning in
December wearing a white robe with a red satin sash tied around my
waist, and a crown of seven candles on my head, carrying a tray that
held warm cinnamon rolls, ginger snaps, and coffee, and singing a
song in Swedish.

But that is one of the things I meant.

One of the most special things about growing up "Swedish" was
the language that my grandparents still spoke whenever it was just
the two of them alone together. I discovered this early on when I
would come downstairs in the morning and they would be sitting in
their kitchen, near the woodstove, talking. As soon as I entered the
room, as if by a magic wand, the language they were speaking would
change from the fascinatingly foreign to the mundane and familiar.

And so I started sneaking up on them. I would tiptoe down the stairs and sit on a lower step listening. Eventually that became a little bit boring so I would begin to slowly poke a little bit of my foot into the room, then withdraw it. And I would continue to do that, a little bit more of my foot each time, until a bemused, bilingual remark about a little *flicka* being awake would precede my full body entering the room.

Both my name and my brother's underwent a wonderful transformation when spoken by my Swedish grandparents: "Yanet" and "Yonny." My sister Betsey, who my mother had refused to name with another name starting with "J" (I wanted her to be named Julia), regretted that there was no difference at all in the way her name was pronounced by them.

My mother had taken a vivid interest in my dad's Swedish heritage, studying Swedish for a time at the university after they were married, and before I was born. It probably did her no more good with my dad than it did me when, in my early twenties I decided I should learn a Germanic language before going off to Europe, and not wanting (at all) to study German, I decided to study Swedish instead. I took a class for a year in evening school at the University of Minnesota. Our teacher was Swedish, a large, jolly, pink-cheeked, full-bearded man. My accent was not bad, and he praised it, but encouraged me to "sing" it more.

I couldn't do that without feeling like I was making fun of my grandparents: it felt like a kind of disloyalty.

But when I tried to speak Swedish with my dad, it was a dead end. He would simply smile and shake his head, and insist that he couldn't understand me. My grandmother had no such problem, and when I told her about my dad's "inability" to understand me (I'm sure he was lying), she sighed a deep sigh, shook her head, and did that characteristic sharp intake of breath, followed by, "*Ach!*...and he was the most Swedish of them all..."

I assume that his refusal to speak Swedish with me had to do with his decision to leave all that behind, typical of the generation that makes the transition required to fully assimilate into a foreign culture. It is true, probably, that he had been "the most Swedish" of his brothers, especially since he was the only one to go to high school, and in order to do so he had boarded with two Swedish women in Cannon Falls during the week. (Both of his brothers did end up with university degrees, one of them with a law degree from Yale; but partly because of farm duties, and partly because of the war, they had been forced to take more circuitous routes, including some correspondence classes, to get their high school degrees).

But my dad didn't completely lose his Swedish roots. My mother, with her interest in his heritage, had proposed "Brita" (a family name) as one of the names for me. "You can't give her a name you can't pronounce," he said, shaking his head.

Then there was the Swedish folk song he loved to sing, "Nikolina," which is a sob story about a young man whose sweetheart's father refuses to give him permission to marry his daughter. He loved to sing that song, and while at the time I had no idea what any of the words meant, I will never forget the sound of them, nor the passion with which he belted out the words as he would stride through our living room singing *"Da gick jag hem och skrev till Nikolina om hon ville vara så ryslight snäll och möta mig nar manen borja skina I ekebacken nasta lordagkvall…"*

The other song he liked to sing was "Oh, if I had the wings of an angel, over these prison walls I would fly…" "Don't you want to be with us, Daddy?" I would ask occasionally when he sang that. But I knew he did. He was a happy man, a very happy man, and he didn't hide it. And—though he was Swedish, and Swedes tend not to show their emotions all that freely—he didn't try to, either.

There was also the extraordinary sense of discretion that was a deeply ingrained part of being Swedish. When I was in college I visited my Swedish grandmother whenever I could, and loved spending time with her. We would sit and talk, about this and about that. One day she told me that she had just learned something about someone in our family that was *so terrible*: **SO, SO terrible,** that she would never be able to tell anyone about it. It was just the **worst thing** she had ever heard, she said, shaking her head, clucking, intaking her breath in that Swedish way, and sighing.

"What was it?!" friends have asked me through the years, eagerly. "Well, I don't know. I didn't ask her," I tell them, to their amazement. But to a girl who was raised in an (even half) Swedish-American home it was quite clear to me that unless Grandma had taken that conversation another step forward herself, this information was not to be shared with me. Hadn't she just told me it was so terrible that she couldn't talk about it?

I did ask my dad about it, years later, after Grandma was no longer alive. I told him about what she had said to me, and asked him what he thought she might have been referring to. One of my grandmother's sisters had been (quite clearly to me, but I wasn't sure it would have been clear to my dad) a lesbian who lived with a very nice woman for many years until "death did them part." I suspected that this might be the scandal my grandmother had been referring to, but I didn't want to suggest that to my dad: I wanted him to tell me what *he* thought it was. "Oh, it was probably the murder," he said, matter-of-factly, to my astonishment. "*Murder?! What murder?!*" I said. I had certainly never heard of a murder in our family. "Oh, there was a barroom brawl, and somebody got killed," he said, still very matter-of-fact. "It wasn't really our family," he added. "It was an in-law."

There was also the time when I was nineteen, and I forgot my journal at my Uncle George's house on Christmas Day. In those days I didn't go anywhere without my journal, and my journal had a great many things in it that I would not have wanted anyone in my family to read. We were already at least a half hour into our drive home that night when I realized, with a horrified clutch in my gut, that I had left it on a table in the living room. "We have to go back," I said. "I forgot my journal." This was a major request, and a terrible waste and inconvenience in my parents' eyes. "We can't have them just send it to you?" my mom asked. "NO," I said, with a vehemence that my father understood, and he turned the car around.

When I knocked on the door and my cousin came to the door to answer it, I told him, with all the dignity and calm I could muster, where I had left my notebook. He brought it to me, and as he handed it to me, he grinned and said, "It's okay, you know. We might have read it; but we wouldn't have been able to *admit* to you that we did, so we couldn't have said anything about it."

As we started our journey homeward for the second time that night, my mother said to me, "You shouldn't write anything you wouldn't want anyone to read." I didn't argue with her, but I knew she was wrong about that too.

* * *

Being Lutheran was an important part of being Swedish-American as well. But the fact that I was raised Lutheran was actually thanks to my mother's mother. My mom had asked her, when she was preparing to marry my dad, what she thought they should do about joining a church. (She had grown up Methodist, so theirs was going to be a "mixed marriage.") "I think Bert would make a better Lutheran than a Methodist," was my grandmother's thoughtful advice.

And she was right. My dad was certainly a "man of faith," but his faith was firmly founded in an intellectual tradition, and I think he would not have been very comfortable with the somewhat closer proximity of Methodism to fundamentalism. (There are Lutheran synods that have flirted with, even embraced fundamentalism; but that was most definitely not part of my father's religious orientation.)

As for me, all through my childhood I longed to be a Catholic. There were the Kennedys, of course, with whom I was fascinated. And our next-door neighbors, when we had moved back to

Minnesota when I was ten, were also Irish Catholics. There were eight children in that family, the last five of them appropriately named Colleen, Michael, Maureen, Kelly, and Patrick. (The first three, Pam, Cindy, and Vicky apparently were named prior to their mother's interest in Irish culture.) I loved all the "high church" details of Catholicism: incense, genuflecting, rosaries, making the sign of the cross. I was envious of all that, as well as of the statuary, the crucifixes (so much more interesting, and more sensual, than our plain crosses); there were the stories of the saints, and all of the other trappings that my mother was so disdainful of. And there was Latin!

But I was happy to at least be a Lutheran, not a Methodist. We often visited the rural Methodist church where my grandparents and my cousins all went to church, so I knew what Methodist services were like. They did a fair amount of singing, which I enjoyed. But they also did weekly responsive readings. That would have been okay had they been read by either pastor or parishioners with an ounce of dramatic emphasis; but they were not, they were droned. At least as Lutherans we didn't have to suffer through responsive readings; and we still had some chanting in Latin as a part of our weekly liturgy, a vestige of Catholicism that I thoroughly enjoyed.

The church we joined when we moved back to Minnesota from Ohio belonged to the American Lutheran Church synod, not the Lutheran Church in America, which was the Scandinavian synod. I don't know if it's for that reason, or for others, that there was a distinct streak of fundamentalist tendencies that existed in the underfabric of that church. For one thing our church participated in the Pioneer Girls, which was a kind of religious version of the Girl Scouts.

I enjoyed being in Pioneer Girls, partly because of the link to American history. Girls would move up the ranks, from Pioneer, to Colonist, to Explorer—which, now that I think about it, is not quite the right order—earning badges along the way. I had a sash full of lovely embroidered badges earned through being able to master the basics of such things as fire building, cookery, and even archery. (The thing I remember most about archery is having a very sore forearm.) I had very little intrinsic interest in most of the skills I was "learning" in order to earn those badges, but I sure loved the badges. I also enjoyed going to the Camp Cherith "sleepaway" camp in northern Minnesota, near Hinckley, for a few years in junior high and high school, first as a camper, later as a counselor's assistant.

I loved going to Camp Cherith, but there was a not very subtle pressure to be "saved" on the last night before each camp session closed that made me uncomfortable. I especially didn't like the pressure to commit my life to Christ, or recommit it, every year. (Wasn't once enough?)

Whoever was behind the fundamentalist strain in our church must have also arranged to take us to see a film, *For Pete's Sake*, at a theatre in downtown Minneapolis sometime in high school; I think I was in tenth grade. It was an event sponsored by the Billy Graham organization. The film was about a man whose life was falling apart (I don't remember exactly how or why, that didn't really matter) who then turned things around by dedicating his life to Christ. At the end of the film we were invited to "come forward" if we also wanted to dedicate our lives to Christ. My Scandinavian Lutheran instincts were strong enough to find all of this a bit strange, but when my best friend whispered "Let's go up there," I agreed, somewhat reluctantly, to do so. (We had to go behind the stage curtain in order to dedicate our lives to Christ, and although I was hesitant, I was also curious to see what was there.)

Immediately upon stepping behind the curtain my friend and I were separated, each of us finding ourselves face to face with an efficient recorder of our conversions. "Are you dedicating your life to Christ, or rededicating?" my interlocutor asked, pencil poised to check the right box on his clipboard. "Well, umm….I don't know. I'm baptized…" I said. (An impeccably Lutheran response.) I don't know which box the recorder then checked, but he went on to offer me a Bible. It was the "Living Bible" version, a new and very loose translation; not a scholarly one. "Oh, I don't need a Bible, we have *so many Bibles* in our house," I demurred. But he pressed the point: "Do you read them?" he asked meaningfully, eyebrow arched, as he pressed the Living Bible into my hands, and checked another box on his clipboard.

The main outcome of this encounter was that I was on the mailing list for *Decision* magazine for many years to come. The handful of tracts I was given that night I kept hidden in the sliding door compartment of the headboard of my bed, as if it were pornography. I knew instinctively that this kind of material was not really my parents' kind of thing. Even my mom, though much less intellectual about her faith than my dad, and with that Methodist upbringing, had always taught me, for example, that "hell is separation from God," a definition that has borne up very well through the years, and seems true to me even now, as more of a secular humanist, or a cultural Christian, than a practicing Lutheran.

When it came time for me to be confirmed, I guess that was when I was about sixteen, we each had an individual consultation with our pastor, at which he dutifully asked us if we had any questions. I had one main question which was, *Can I just skip this step for now?* I did not feel ready to make what I considered to be a serious commitment to Lutheranism at precisely the moment in my intellectual life when I was beginning to question so much about it. (Well, actually I had begun much earlier. But I hadn't had to take a *vow* before then; I hadn't had to solemnly and publicly affirm that I believed in it.)

But I knew that if I declined, it would be a massive disappointment to my family; most of all to my mother. (I think my dad would have understood, perhaps even approved.) So I decided to skip that drama, and just take the vows.

When a few years later my mother accused me of not honoring my confirmation vows by not wanting to go to church anymore, I protested. "I took those vows because I felt pressure to do so," I said. "I think confirmation should not come at that age, it should be a bit later, when people have had a chance to think about it more." My mother disagreed, pointing out that when young adults went away to college, they often became "confused" by exposure to new ways of thinking.

Well, that was kind of my point. But I didn't argue it any further. I knew it would be too painful for her.

Still, I think even my mother took a kind of vicarious pleasure in the new theological thinking I went about exploring when I got to college. When I was a freshman in college, home for the Easter break, the phone rang in the middle of a heated post-dinner discussion I was having with my Uncle George. I had stated the (heretical to him) point of view that I didn't think Christ's *literal* resurrection from the dead was all that important; it was Christ's *teachings* that mattered, I said; and the kind of life he called on his followers to live. "Without the resurrection the whole religion falls apart, there's no meaning to it!" he protested, and that is when the phone rang. It was my roommate calling me. "Oh, hold on for a minute, Wendy," my mother, who had answered the phone, said. "She's here, but she's arguing about religion with her uncle." When I got to the phone Wendy asked me, in a bemused tone of voice, "Janet, what are you doing to those poor people? And on Easter!"

Well, it is just as I once said to James Emanuel, an expatriate African-American poet whose work the beloved Parisian bookseller Odile Hellier had introduced me to when I was teaching literature in Paris. James became a good friend after I invited him to come and read his poetry to my students every year, over a period of years. He was, if not an atheist, an avowed anti-established-religionist, with very good reason. (He was once denied entry into the vestibule of a "white" church in Washington DC during an air raid drill, during World War II, *by the minister*.)

Once, remembering my early grapplings with the presumed superiority of Christianity over other religions, I said to him, "I asked a lot of good questions, but I never got any good answers."

He laughed that wonderful laugh he had; and I always loved making him laugh.

Coon Rapids Senior High

When I think about the person who inhabited my body for most of my high school years, it feels like that was someone else. When I remember being five, ten, up until about twelve years old, the person I remember having those experiences, those thoughts, those feelings was *me*.

The person who took over after that, until I got to college, however, was someone else.

I don't think this was anyone's fault: it was just an aspect, at least for me it was an aspect, of adolescence. It is why the girl who would have naturally gravitated to being involved in school plays (for example) became instead an avid basketball fan. (Our school had a very good basketball team, and I had crushes on the star players.)

So I went to the games with my friends, and they were often very exciting. I would come home from them full of details to tell my dad, who would listen patiently to my play-by-play accounts of jump shots and free throws, of who did what when, my indignation over ridiculous calls by the referee. He never let on that any of it was less than interesting to him. But it had to be. Still, I think he appreciated my genuine enthusiasm for the game.

I still like watching basketball. (Well, if I *have to* watch a sport, that is one of the ones I would choose, along with baseball. I call them the "balletic" sports.)

During those years my dream—a dream I never even tried for—would have been to be a cheerleader. Being incapable of doing the splits *at all* I knew I had to be content with being friends with some of the cheerleaders. I did try out for the drill team, the "Cardettes," one year. They wore short red velvet uniforms with white satin pleated insets; and black fishnet stockings with ballet shoes to show off their high kicks; and they carried pompoms, so they were *almost* like cheerleaders. I nearly made it, but alas, in the end I was not chosen. That was a bitter disappointment to me at the time, though my mom was probably relieved that she wasn't going to have to drive me to school every morning to get me there by seven o'clock for practices, instead of letting me take the school bus.

I'm riding the school bus, sitting next to my friend Colleen who lives next door. I've been reading Rebecca by Daphne De Maurier and each morning on the way to school I tell her about "what happened next." She's a wonderful listener, fascinated to hear the story unfold, and full of all the right questions at all the right moments. She's really one of my best friends though we are in completely separate social circles at school. But she's always there for me when push comes to shove, and ours is a friendship that will be for life. Once during high school we are studying together for a final exam in math, and for some reason I completely forget how to do everything! I'm in general a stronger student than she is, even in math, or at least I get better grades, which is of course not always the same thing. But I seem to have hit a wall the night before the test and I have become completely unable to do even the simplest calculations. "Oh Janet, what's happened to you?" she giggles, incredulous, but she doesn't waste time with that, just calmly, gently leads me through the steps of how to borrow, or carry over, or divide, or whatever it is I've forgotten how to do.

Coon Rapids was white, *very* white, which is why I was puzzled when one day our school bus arrived at the high school and we all noticed that someone had burned the words "N---- Falls" into one of the exterior yellow brick walls. There was one—one!—light-skinned black student in our school. He was a good basketball player, and he was very handsome, thus he was quite popular. Why would someone have done such a thing as to call us a name like that? It just didn't make any sense to me. (I had never heard of black people being referred to as "coons" and didn't, in fact, until years later, which is a credit I guess, not only to my family but to everyone I spent time with back then.)

I remember going to one basketball game at Mechanic Arts High School in St. Paul. This was a largely black inner-city school, and the cheerleaders there made quite an impression on all of us that night. "Go *back*! Go *back*! Go back in the woods! Your team ain't nothin' and your coach is no good..." they taunted.

We were all a bit nonplussed. We hadn't heard a cheer like that before! There had been a bit of tension on the school bus riding to that game—was this a dangerous thing to do, to go to a game in *that* neighborhood, at night? But those teasing cheers were the extent of any "trouble."

Minnesota public schools were pretty good, and though Coon Rapids was mostly a working-class suburb—many of my friends' parents worked in factories, or drove trucks, or did other blue-collar jobs—the college prep track in our high school was not bad. There were four languages offered—French, Spanish, German, and Latin. I studied French of course, because it was the most beautiful language I had ever heard.

I took only the strict requirements for math and science—which took me through Higher Algebra (where I met my Waterloo with logarithms); and Chemistry. Our chemistry teacher had quintessential science teacher looks—he was thin and he wore wire-rim glasses before they were fashionable; he had owly eyes, and pallid skin. He required absolute precision in our lab reports, including such superficial details as the margins, which had to be accurate to within an eighth of an inch. My experiments *never* went well, which meant that when I calculated the margin of error it was usually an astronomical figure. "That's correct," he would assure me when I expressed dismay at my results. "You have correctly calculated your margin of error." "Yes, but it's 150,000 percent," I would mumble, in disgust. It didn't bother Mr. Krug though. He often told us that one day we would thank him for being such a strict teacher; and through the years, though I have often thought of him with a kind of affection, I have never once really *thanked* him. I suppose I should thank him for letting me know, through all that emphasis on scientific precision, that I should never consider any career that would involve dealing with chemistry.

In Higher Algebra I somehow got the highest grade in the school on the final exam (the "somehow" was, I am sure, the fact that it was a multiple-choice test, and I had devised a fairly effective system for guessing). When Mr. Hewitt announced the honor, he added, "If I didn't know you better, I'd say you cheated," with a suppressed grin. "Because I *know* you didn't understand this material," he added. I didn't deny it: he was right! And I was just happy that I didn't have to take Precalculus. Or Physics. Also that he knew me well enough to know I wouldn't cheat.

The only theater I was involved in during high school was in ninth grade, when all freshmen were required to take a Speech class. (The topic I chose for my persuasive speech was "Why We Must Abolish the Electoral College." *Ahem.*) For our drama unit we were either assigned to act out a scene from *The Glass Menagerie*, or we selected it, I don't remember which. I was given (or assigned myself) the role of Amanda, and learned a scene with two classmates, both of whom were nice enough, but neither were very natural actors. We presented the scene in which Amanda blows up at Tom and he storms out of the house, accidentally knocking some of Laura's precious glass animals off of the shelf, and breaking them, on his way out.

It was not the most satisfying experience for someone with real fire in her blood for theater, as I had. Every time during rehearsals when "Laura" was fondling one of the animals on the shelf, and I snapped my line at her ("What are you *doing*?!"), startled by the intensity of my voice, she would instantly break out of her role, and say "I'm supposed to pick this up at this point…" And when during our performance for the class, "Tom" missed *accidentally* knocking the animals from the shelf by catching them with the jacket he was grabbing, he turned around, came back to the shelf and very deliberately knocked them down ferociously one by one, giggling as he did so.

I, as Amanda, could only sigh and wish to be with more sophisticated partners.

I graduated in 1971, just before the effect of the "sixties" began to really be felt in the general culture. So, at that time girls still took a year of required "Home Ec" and boys took a required year of "Shop." (It would have been much more practical and helpful had the requirements been switched of course: but no one was thinking that way, not yet, not then.)

In Home Ec we learned how to sew in one semester; and how to cook and plan meals in the other. I didn't mind sewing: in fact, that foreign personality that dwelt within me for my high school years took to it quite enthusiastically for a few years. I sewed a lot of my own clothing and loved shopping for fabric. I hated hemming, though, and usually convinced my mom to do that part with the transparent flattery of "Oh Mom you do this so much better than I do…" Good sport that she was, she almost always obliged, and would stay up late hemming whatever dress or skirt I had just made for me before she went to bed.

The cooking part of the curriculum was apparently designed with meals from *Ozzie and Harriet*, or *Father Knows Best*, or *Leave it to Beaver* in mind. Our home was nothing like the homes depicted in those TV shows, and my mom's style of serving dinner did not match any of the four standard "serving styles" we were taught about in that class. She also never dressed like the moms in those shows, in a prim and proper shirtwaist dress, with pearls around her neck, looking like she'd come straight from the hairdresser. And she certainly did not set the table for breakfast the night before, before she went to bed, as we were advised good homemakers would do. (When she did not fall asleep exhausted in an armchair, she used that time to read. Or to hem the dresses I had sewn.)

Summers were filled with various wholesome—and fun— activities. We had a youth pastor at our church, a short and very dynamic young Italian-American from New Jersey with an equally petite (and charming, and sweet) wife. His name was Ernie Mancini, and he brought wonderful and infectious energy to his work. He got us inspired to create a youth "drop-in" center at the church; and several times he took us to a Lutheran camp in the Black Hills called Outlaw Ranch. We would go there in a rented school bus, stopping at various points of interest in South Dakota along the way: he got us singing, and clapping, and generally rejoicing. And he kept us out of trouble.

I was also in the marching band, playing the clarinet. Our band director was a very dedicated, and I think probably quite talented, or at least serious, musician. It must have been frustrating for him to deal with the kind of shenanigans that are so typical in high schools. I remember one day after a particularly boisterous class I needed to ask him something after class and when I went back into the music room to do so he was standing by the piano, resting his elbow on the top of it and looking toward the window. It seemed to me that as he turned toward me, there were tears in his eyes. Still, he got things out of kids musically that surpassed all expectations, that's for sure, and we particularly excelled in our marching band. We went all around the state to march in various parades, and even a couple of times to Thunder Bay, Canada; and we brought home a lot of trophies. The uniforms we wore were black wool suits, with a heavy white cotton overlay with a cardinal, our school mascot, stitched upon the breast. And tall fake hats in the style of the guards at Buckingham Palace. The uniforms were, in other words, VERY HOT! Before each parade, we were given salt pills to keep us from keeling over as we waited to take our position in the parade, but every once in a while someone did anyway.

I had a fairly active and satisfactory social life, though I was always pining after boys who were not at all interested in me, mostly basketball players. I only went on a couple of dates in high school, with nice boys in whom I had no interest. Well, I had interest in one of them; but then he quickly lost interest in me, which was both heartbreaking and a relief, because dating was excruciatingly awkward. I think it probably still is: in all the years that have followed high school, I have certainly never missed it, and wouldn't mind if I never do it again. I think of it as a kind of job interview for love; and who would ever want to go on a job interview if there were any other way of getting a job?

I graduated with a very large graduating class—635 I believe. And even though it was very large, the guidance counselors at the school had an individual meeting with each and every student prior to graduation. There had been a memorable moment during my senior year meeting with my counselor. "What are your plans for next year?" he asked me, pen in hand, ready to mark down my list of colleges. "I'm thinking of going to Australia," I said, and I will never forget the look of shock that passed across his face. He literally paled. "My dear, you must go to college," he said, softly, but emphatically, shaking his head in either disbelief or dismay. "Oh, I'm going to go to college, just not *next* year," I replied, confidently. My parents were both graduates of the University of Minnesota, and I had always assumed that I would be a college graduate too.

But since the majority of my classmates would be going on to trade schools or community colleges, not universities, I later realized that probably what he saw was the possibility of an academically gifted student falling off the college track and ending up working in a factory somewhere, and he was horrified at the thought. He convinced me that I should *not* go to a wedding in Australia with my cousins the following year, as I had been contemplating doing, but that instead I should take advantage of the opportunity to get scholarships aimed at graduating seniors, and stay on the academic path.

It was a convincing argument, and I decided to do what he suggested.

But I did *not* do what he no doubt would have thought I should do after my freshman year, which was to continue on for three more years, and graduate; and then get a good job.

Becoming Myself Again

In high school the "me" that was not really me was the one who wished I could be a cheerleader, and who fantasized about marrying a high school basketball coach and living the life of a suburban housewife (but! the wife of a basketball coach!) in a suburb much like Coon Rapids. (As I write these words it seems even to me that they can't possibly be true. But they are!)

It was after high school that I began the bumpy road back to being myself again. But it took a while.

For a while I bounced from college to college, something you could do in those days, back in the early 1970s when even private school educations were somewhat affordable for middle-class, or even lower-middle-class, students with good grades. I started out at Concordia College, in Moorhead, Minnesota, just across the river from Fargo, North Dakota. I had applied to several private Lutheran colleges in Minnesota; I think those are the only places I applied to, and though I would have preferred to go to any of the others that I had applied to, the package of financial aid offered by Concordia was by far the most generous. Later I realized this was largely because, in a time of significant social change, unlike the other schools to which I had been applying, Concordia had kept its social atmosphere, and its role of *in loco parentis,* firmly entrenched in the 1950s, which made the parents of incoming students, and the alumni, feel more comfortable. Concordia had therefore hung onto its donor base much better than schools that were listening to the call of the 1960s, and abandoning their attempts to regulate student behavior. Or so it apparently seemed to the alumni and administration of Concordia. Thus they had more money to offer incoming students.

I only stayed there for a year and a half, a year and a half that I will never regret not only because I made some of my closest lifelong friends there, but because I had an excellent academic experience. The academics were not the problem. The other students were not the problem. The problem was that the rigid and oppressive, joyless administration saw sin and sex everywhere. To be fair, when talking about students in their late teens, of course sex *is* everywhere. And this was the post-pill and pre-AIDS era. So yes, a lot of the kids in my generation *were* sleeping around, though I personally was not doing that. We were also smoking marijuana and doing other drugs too, and of course drinking heavily. At Concordia we probably did even more of this than we would have been doing had we not been placed in an adversarial position with the administration of the college by their overly strict, and often very unfair, rules.

"Why is it that girls have a curfew and boys do not?" we asked college administrators, reasonably enough. "Well, if the girls all go to their rooms, so will the boys," they replied. But they were ignoring the fact that less than half a mile away, at Moorhead State College, both boys and girls were carrying on until all hours with no curfew for either sex.

I think the moment I knew I was probably going to have to leave was at the all-college community meeting at which the topic of passionate discussion was why our "inter-visitation" hours—those hours when boys and girls were allowed to visit each other in their dorm rooms—had to be so restrictive. (Every other Sunday from 1-4 p.m. DOORS OPEN!!!) When someone at that meeting protested the open-door rule as presenting an unjustifiable lack of respect for privacy, the college president reddened and, with a shaking voice proclaimed, "There is NO WAY that a young man and a young woman can be together in the same room for more than THREE HOURS with the door closed, without all standards of decency being completely abandoned."

I knew for a fact it was perfectly possible for such a situation to fail to descend into anything like what he was suggesting, and remember reflecting on a couple of situations I'd been in and thinking, "If only..."

But the real problem for me was that this struggle with the administration of the college is where our energies were being focused. My friends on other campuses were spending their activist energy on things that seemed far more important to me. For example, protesting the Vietnam War.

And so I started spending more and more time away from Moorhead, going to Minneapolis on weekends, staying with my friends there, participating in antiwar marches.

The other enormous waste of energy was the necessity of getting around all those rules. For of course we had to, didn't we? Put a fence around someone, and it is almost inevitable that they will start devoting a great deal of energy trying to figure out how to get over, around, or under it. And so that is what we did. We couldn't return to our dorms after a certain hour without suffering consequences, so we would stay out all night. (We were able to do this because, it being the 1970s after all, at least they did not do bed checks.) A few of my girlfriends and I developed a sort of secondary home in a dorm where a few of our male friends shared a suite; we called it the "Brown Hotel." There we would smoke marijuana, talk until all hours, then sleep uncomfortably on the floor, in chairs, in various beds, until it was late enough in the morning to find our way back to our own dorms, and our own beds. Honestly, many of those nights I would have been much happier back in my own room at a decent hour (but after curfew!), reading.

I had been asked on entering Concordia, the first day of orientation, to declare my major. "Undecided," I said. "No, you must choose a major," I was told. "Okay, French," I replied. It seemed as good as any, and I did love studying French. The trouble came when toward the end of my freshman year I went to sign up for my sophomore classes. "I don't see any French classes here," my (French professor) advisor said. "I'm not taking any French this time," I said. "You can't do that: you're a French major!" he said, and once again I felt cornered.

And so it was inevitable that I would leave. At my exit interview with my French professor, who was very sorry to see me go, he tried to talk me out of it. "Why do you want to leave?" he asked. "I dunno, it's just...it's a little isolated here," I said. "There's not enough to do..." "Judy Collins was here last week," he said, and cruelly (but honestly), I replied with an impatient shake of the head, "I really don't like Judy Collins that much." He even tried to entice me to stay by offering me a summer job at Concordia Language Villages if I would stick with the program. But I knew I needed to go. (Many years later, when my son Phineas spent a summer working as a counselor at the Concordia Language Villages in the French language village, I felt that something had come full circle in a wonderful kind of way.)

I knew I had to leave Concordia. But I didn't have a very clear picture of what I wanted to do with my life. I knew I wanted to travel. I knew I loved to write. But during my college years I was still strongly influenced by a group of friends from my high school who had developed an enthusiasm for the "back to the land" movement that was popular in the early 1970s. For some of my friends this was the right path, and some of them ended up following it and living good and admirable "back to the land" lives.

And of course, looking back from the vantage point of 2022, it's pretty clear that it would have been good for everyone on the planet if more people had engaged in a more organic way of life, whether in an urban or a rural setting—if more people had found a more harmonious way of living on the earth.

But "back to the land" wasn't the right path for me. Still, I tried to develop an enthusiasm for it. Part of the reason for this no doubt had to do with a boy I was in love with who had no interest in me, except "as a friend." He was in the circle of friends who were very taken with the idea of buying land, building log cabins on it, learning how to garden, can tomatoes, and the like. One day I expressed regret (or something similar) to one of the young women in that group, that I hadn't yet learned to can tomatoes. "You could do so if you didn't spend so much time writing," she said.

Did I imagine that she pronounced the word "writing" with a bit of disdain, or disapproval? I don't think I imagined it, because I remember that her words hit me like a jolt. It felt like an aggression, and I think it was. But in a way it was also a gift, I suppose. Because in that moment I knew with all my heart and soul that I needed to distance myself from anyone who would try to steer me away from writing.

That perhaps was a first step toward my becoming (again) who I was really meant to be.

* * *

There was one very nice boy at Concordia who was in love with me. He was smart, funny, sweet, a talented musician, and he adored me. I liked him a lot; but he was far more ready for a serious relationship than I was. I wanted to travel, and so did he; I think he would have liked to travel with me. But he also wanted to possess me, and I was not at all ready to be possessed, except by the boy I was in love with. And so he gave up on me, and found someone else. I regret that we weren't able to maintain a friendship, but I do understand it.

During my on-again, off-again college years (I went to three different schools before finally graduating from the University of Minnesota like the rest of my family), I became involved with a couple of different "bad boys," and to this day I don't really know why. I guess they were exotic. They certainly weren't going to tie me down.

He's a very good-looking alcoholic with beautiful, sparkly blueish-gray bedroom eyes and a poetic name. He's obsessed with an unrequited love, and I am for some reason if not exactly obsessed with him, certainly wasting a lot of time following him around. What is his appeal, other than the fact that he calls me "Moonbeam"? I'm not sure. He asks me one night why I don't want to spend my time with my real boyfriend. "He loves you; I don't," he says, not unkindly, as he gently places a stray lock of hair behind my ear. He's speaking the truth. I don't know what to say: I don't know the answer to the question.

Thanks to some lucky breaks and my guardian angels I managed to come through that period of my life relatively unscathed. Not everyone is so lucky.

The only real regret I have about that period—because I *was* lucky that I suffered none of the disastrous outcomes that could have befallen me from engaging in some of the risky behavior I did—is that I wasted so much time hanging around smoky bars waiting for those "bad boys" to show up, or to finish playing pool so I could go home with them.

It was time that could have been *so* much better spent reading.

"The Problem of Sustenance"

One of my favorite lines in Hemingway's memoir of his youthful years in Paris, *A Moveable Feast*, is a quote by his friend Evan Shipman. Hemingway recounts a conversation they were having about this and about that, about all the things they hoped to do, or planned to do, or somesuch; the kind of conversation brilliant young writers struggling to get started, or to keep going, tend to have. At a certain point Shipman pauses and says, "Of course, there is the problem of sustenance."

I solved the problem of sustenance in a number of ways before I finally found my path, or accepted my role in life, or however you want to say that. In one of his essays James Baldwin wrote that the American writer "fights his way to one of the lowest rungs on the American social ladder by means of pure bull-headedness and an indescribable series of odd jobs." I was lucky in this regard too. Most of my jobs were not all that odd.

Unlike many of my friends, I never had to work as a waitress, and it's a good thing too. I would have been a *terrible* waitress, and would consequently have probably not gotten very good tips. I would have been very pleasant, as pleasant as pleasant could be. But I would have forgotten almost every single thing that I was asked to do. Several times! I suspect I also would not have had the physical grace and strength required to do the job well. So whatever tips I would have gotten would have only been from very kind people who felt sorry for me.

During high school, with my mother's urging, even pressure, I got a job at the local library, which was a natural for me, I guess, and not a bad job. I also did some babysitting, but I never liked babysitting very much. It was scary, having to stay awake late at night in someone else's house, waiting for the parents to come home. There were stories in the newspapers both in Cincinnati when we had still lived there, and later in Minnesota, about abducted babysitters whose decomposed bodies ended up being found in the woods, or in a ditch somewhere, months later. I remember in one of the homes where I babysat, sitting in a recliner chair that I carefully positioned facing away from the "peek" windows in the front door, so that anyone looking in wouldn't be able to see me (though I wouldn't be able to see them either, sitting like that); and trying to stay awake watching some dumb TV show while I waited for the parents to get home, and hoping that they wouldn't have been drinking.

Why didn't I read then too?

My college work-study job at Concordia was in the cafeteria, where I emptied dirty trays coming along the conveyor belt between the dining room and the kitchen, working side by side with international students from Africa, or maybe the Caribbean. The nature of the job didn't allow for a lot of small talk, really, so I'm not sure where they were from: it was too noisy to talk!

The most unpleasant job I ever had was in a plastics factory in Fridley, one of the suburbs adjacent to Coon Rapids. That was a summer job between my freshman and sophomore years in college. I worked there with three other high school friends who were also in college. The national Occupational Safety and Health Administration (OSHA) had only been established a year earlier, and probably no one who worked there knew enough to call OSHA. But what a horrible place to work! The place where we took our obligatory fifteen-minute morning and afternoon breaks, and also ate our lunches, was right in the middle of the deafening sound of the machines, which kept pounding away, of course, as people took turns eating at a grease-stained table. The "foreman" of the factory was a sexy looking German woman who strolled around the place in her miniskirts and high-heeled shoes making sure everyone was working at an impossible pace: when she saw that someone was managing to more or less keep up with the pace of the machines, she would increase the speed. My worst day there was with the plastic canister machine: you were supposed to open a very heavy door, remove four (very hot!) canisters from the mold—without protective gloves. Then you were to stack them, and once they had cooled a bit, pack them into cardboard packing cartons, all of this quickly enough so that you could open the door in time to take the next four canisters out, before the plastic started dripping around the edges of the mold. I couldn't go fast enough to do the packing part, so there I stood, surrounded by mounting piles of plastic canisters reaching toward the ceiling, looking a bit like Charlie Chaplin in *Modern Times*, or Lucille Ball working on the assembly line in the candy factory. I don't remember what the forewoman said when she saw my predicament: I do remember that she was not at all sympathetic.

The other thing that was not so much unpleasant, but just sad about that job was the gulf that existed between us four college students and the other workers. We knew very well that we were only there for the summer, and so did they. For us it was a great reminder of why getting a college degree was a good idea. I'm not sure what it was for them. A lot of them were probably going to spend many years of their lives in that godawful place. They weren't unfriendly toward us, but surely they must have had complicated, or at least slightly ambivalent, feelings about our presence there. One of my friends dealt with the stress of the situation by frequently breaking into not-very-well-controlled, bordering on hysterical, giggling. What must they have thought? What was so damn funny?

Later, when I had quit college for the second time and was living in the college town of Mankato, I applied for a job at a printing business whose main product was wedding invitations. I didn't even find out exactly what that job would have been, because I decided midway through the interview that I didn't want it, right after I had been told what the hourly pay was (very low!) and had been asked if I would be willing to work weekends. I knew I could do better than that, and I wanted to spend many of my weekends in Minneapolis, so I found a way to somehow politely wriggle out of the interview, and left with a huge sense of relief that I didn't take *that* job.

I also had a brief period of employment—just a month or two—right after I had dropped out of college for the first time, when I worked at a company called Standard Fabrics in Minneapolis, in a warehouse downtown by the river. I remember the cold, and the smell of linseed oil in the air as I would walk to work early in the January mornings, from the house where I was living with friends, on 2nd Ave Southeast, over the Hennepin Avenue Bridge. My job was stapling swatches of fabric to advertising flyers. Despite the menial nature of the job, I remember that there was a fair amount of tension about doing it right. When after a month or so of that job I wanted to join some friends from college on a skiing trip to Montana, I asked my supervisor for a week off (unpaid). I was told no, and told that furthermore, if I went on my trip, there would be no job for me when I returned. I knew I could do better than that too, so I quit and went with my friends to Montana. There was a nice young woman I worked with at Standard Fabrics, her name was Marsha. She was a bit older than me, kind, and clearly way too intelligent to be doing that job. I thought of her as being very sophisticated, since she was living with her boyfriend. I wonder what happened to her.

Fortunately, I knew how to type, and I was a very good typist. I am of a generation of women, born in the 1950s, many of whom were told *not* to learn to type, for fear of the fate that might relegate them to. It was well-meaning advice and perhaps not always the worst advice in the world. But this advice was not given to me; in fact my mother encouraged me to learn to type, thinking it was a valuable practical skill to have, and she was *so right* about that. That was one of the most useful things I learned in high school.

The rest of my jobs during college, and for a while after college, were all typing jobs. When I came back from Montana I learned about a "temp" agency at the University of Minnesota, and I got a steady series of temporary jobs, some of them quite interesting, that way. I worked for a while for the coaches of the university basketball, baseball, and track teams; the track coach, Roy Griak, was the nicest one. I also worked for the chair of the Psychology Department, and one day when I was working there Starke Hathaway, a former department chair and one of the authors of the MMPI, came striding, almost bouncing, into the office. He was a handsome older gentleman with a kind of rugged charm; I remember that he was sporting slightly soiled basketball shoes and a well-worn flight jacket.

The most interesting place I worked at the university, I would have to say, was the Program in Human Sexuality, which was within the university's medical school. This was a quintessentially 1970s kind of place. The program was a joint venture of the university's medical school and Lutheran Social Services. The fundamental idea behind the teaching and training that went on there was that health care professionals, clergy, therapists, and anyone else to whom a person might confide a sexual problem or "deviancy" should at the very least learn not to look horrified or shocked when their clients (or parishioners, or patients) found the courage to confess their problem to them—but rather would be able to remain calm and nonjudgmental, and find a way to help and support the person, or perhaps convince them that it wasn't as much of a problem as they thought.

One of the ways this "desensitization" of professionals was done was through a "Sexual Attitude Reassessment" seminar, during which a multimedia presentation of sexually explicit imagery would be projected on a screen. Afterward, in small groups the attendees would discuss their feelings about what they had seen; try to become comfortable with using blunt and explicit language about sexuality; and learn about the wide range of normal and abnormal sexual behaviors.

I met my first really serious boyfriend there. He had been hired to work with the AV team on creating the slide show montages for these seminars, which were a key part of the program's curriculum. He was a New Yorker, born and raised in the West Village by his

Puerto Rican single mom, but educated at a boarding school in the Berkshires and later at Bard College. He was one of the smartest people I'd ever known, and also the most sensitive, and generous. He had a brilliant wit, was a wonderful storyteller, and had an amazing ability to recite favorite passages from various works of literature verbatim. He fell deeply in love with me and I fell in love with him too, though not as deeply. (I was still carrying a torch for the boy who wasn't at all interested in me.) He took me often to a restaurant called the Cork and Cleaver in Golden Valley, a suburb of Minneapolis, where we would eat crab drenched in a rich butter sauce. He introduced me to vermouth as an aperitif, and Drambuie as a digestif, and we talked for hours, about books, about politics, and the rest was just storytelling of our own, about our own lives. He was the best teacher of literature I've ever had, and ever will have, even though he is not really a teacher at all.

There were many interesting things about working in that place, and many interesting people who worked there. I made a few life-long friends among them. One of them was the program manager, who although she was one of the more conventional members of the team, and the most organized, was also lenient enough to allow me and one of my friends there to take our lunch breaks at Cedar Lake in the summertime. This involved allowing us to take longish breaks, since we had to drive about fifteen minutes to get to the lake, and back again. Not to mention that on our return we looked like we had just been swimming halfway across a lake, which we had been! Nobody seemed to think anything about this was all that unusual, though: when we were working we did good work, and that was all that was expected of us. If only more workplaces, more office managers, could be the same, what a happy world this could be!

The director of the program was a medical doctor, a pediatrician. He was a nice man, and he had a kind of charismatic charm for many people; but to me it seemed there was also something a bit "off" about him, even aside from the excessively romantic visionary he was. You could see it in his eyes, and in the vacancy of his smile. He had bought a huge historic red brick neo-Classical house—a small mansion, really—on Summit Avenue in St. Paul, where he lived with his girl-friend and several of the people he had brought in from around the country to work on creative projects at the program, including my New Yorker boyfriend. The director's former wife and her current partner lived in the spacious attic apartment, and a talented young poet from nearby Macalester College rented—or, knowing the direc-tor and his generosity, perhaps simply lived in—the carriage house.

Eventually—not surprisingly—the academic contingent of the program became uncomfortable with the visionary contingent, espe-cially (I think) with the director's dubious skills in financial manage-ment—and the program was moved from the medical school into another division of the university, leaving most of the visionary con-tingent looking for new jobs. Because I knew how to type, I landed on my feet immediately. I just got another job typing at the university.

One of the places I worked was in the University Hospital's Pharmacy Department, and I also worked for a while in—I *think* it was in—the Department of Civil Engineering. I had a really nice boss there, who offered me a permanent job. It was a good job he was offer-ing: good salary, excellent benefits. Had I taken that job, a civil service position with room for growth at the University of Minnesota, I could have led a life that was much more stable than the one I've led: I could have relatively soon bought a house, a car, maybe even a lake cabin one day. But I didn't want that. I wanted to go to Europe. And so, I thanked my boss, but told him no, I was sorry, but I just didn't want to do that. "I'm offering you a really good job" he said, brow furrowed, a look of concern in his eyes. After all, I was twenty-five by then, old enough to start settling down and get serious about something. "I know it's a good job," I said, "And I really appreciate the offer." "But" (I repeated), "I want to go to Europe." "Why don't you go to Europe and then come back and work here?" he said. I just shook my head. He didn't understand. I didn't want to go to Europe on a timetable. I wanted to go there and see what might happen. I wanted to leave room for that.

Into the Wider World

On the ferry between Dover and Calais c. 1979

From the time I knew there was a place called France, I had wanted to go there. When I was a little girl, in my mind France was a place where kings and queens lived in castles situated in lovely, verdant valleys. As I became a little bit older, I became vaguely aware that it was a place where they spoke a language so beautiful the words had a kind of sensuality about them. (This was before I knew the word "sensuality.") I studied French in high school and college, and by the time I had dropped out of

Concordia, and was living temporarily back in Coon Rapids with my parents, the desire to go to France was beginning to become a quiet, desperate, and unhealthy obsession. I knew this one Sunday afternoon when, as I was walking along the road to visit a friend half a mile away, I found myself muttering to myself, over and over, the delicious words *"le roi du coeur, le roi du coeur, le roi du coeur"* practically the whole way there. I had seen the film of the same name in Minneapolis the night before and could not let go of those lovely words, nor of the pleasure of speaking them aloud. "Either I am going to have to get over there," I announced, to myself, aloud, in English, "Or *I* am going to become a lunatic."

But it was a while before I was able to get there. Flying to Europe was very expensive in the late 1970s, and for someone who was earning her living as a typist, even while living at home with her parents, being able to save enough money to buy the plane ticket was going to take a while.

That is why I was so excited when, one day in 1977 Dan Rather announced on the CBS Evening News that a Sir Freddy Laker had just started a no-frills airline that was offering flights from New York to London for the unheard-of price of $135. "Okay, that's it," I muttered to myself as I listened to the rest of the story. "Now I can do it."

Getting over there was now feasible, but I knew that once I got there I would want to be able to stay for a while. So I decided, then and there, that I would work and save as much money as I could for the next year, and leave for Europe the following September. I began to plan with a girlfriend to leave one year later.

To his credit, my boyfriend, who was about fifteen years older than me, and who had everything to lose and probably not much to gain in encouraging me in this venture, was very supportive of my plan. Not once did he use his considerable powers of persuasion to try to dissuade me from stepping out into the world on my own. On the contrary, when the time came to go a year later and the girlfriend was unable to join me, I hesitated: he urged me on, and drove me to New York to catch the plane. ("You need to do this," he said. "You can do this." And he was right, on both counts.)

The only influence he tried to exert regarding my plan, was that just before I left he sang the praises of his beloved London long and hard enough that he convinced me I really ought to stay there for at least a few days before going on to France. (He also gave me the *Blue Guide* to London, thinking that might help seal the argument.) Fervent anglophile that he was, and nothing if not eloquent, he convinced me to do so, and I didn't regret it. I stayed with the friend of a friend who was studying at the London School of Economics and who had a shared flat in Earl's Court. We went to the theater, the symphony, we ate wonderful Indian food together, he helped me plan my trip. It was a lot of fun, and London was wonderful, but it was not my destination: within a week I was on my way to France.

There was no "chunnel" then, and no Eurostar train—in 1978, the choices of Channel crossings were all by boat, either from Dover to Calais or from Newhaven to Dieppe. The plan I came up with, with my London friend's help, was to make my assault on *la belle France* gradually, warming up my untested French language skills in the friendlier territory of Normandy before attacking the capital. So it was that I took the longer channel crossing, from Newhaven to Dieppe, where there was a youth hostel I planned to stay at the first night. As the overnight boat drew near to the shore, people began to leave their benches and make for the exits. I saw one young man— an archeologist fresh from a dig was my guess, judging from his deep and even tan—leave his seat, a seat which offered a prime view of the Dieppe harbor, and I slipped into it the moment he had vacated it. So it was with surprise that, a few minutes later, I saw that the same young man was back, wheeling a bicycle. "Oh, did I steal your seat?" I asked, apologetically. "Oh, it's okay," he said. He was nothing if not gallant. We struck up a short and unremarkable conversation, one young traveling American to another, and then we went on our separate ways. I didn't expect to ever see him again, nor did the thought occur to me that I wouldn't.

That was our close encounter of the first kind. Fleeting, on a boat.

The second encounter came later that same day, in the youth hostel. I had found my way there using the public bus system in Dieppe, and was feeling quite pleased with myself despite the gloomy weather. I arrived at the hostel before it was open for the day, and was invited to wait in a kind of storage shed adjacent to the main hall, where I could keep out of the rain. I was sitting there, resting and absorbing the fact that I really was in France—the bus driver had taken my money, and said *Voila!* as he gave me my ticket—when the door opened, and there was the same young American, wheeling his bicycle. "Hunh! You again," he remarked, in an unenthusiastic but not unfriendly tone; a comment that I echoed. He sat down on the uncovered mattress of the cot across from me, took a bar of chocolate out of his backpack—it was Milka chocolate, with a lovely lavender wrapper. He cocked his head inquisitively at me, then asked, "Would you like a piece of chocolate?" "Oh, I'm afraid I would," I replied, with a smile.

There were very few guests in the hostel that night. Steve—for that was his name—asked me if I would like to go grocery shopping and then share a meal with him. I accepted his invitation, and we went to the nearest *supermarché*—a Monoprix? Prisunic? In the dairy aisle, he picked up a quart of milk. "*Lait frais,*" he read. "Wow! Strawberry milk!" Being of a generation where most women still felt that the polite thing was to pretend that men were smarter than they were, I felt caught in a bind. "Mmm," I said, diplomatically, "I *think* that means 'fresh.'" "Oh no," he replied, with complete confidence. "I know very few words in French but I do know that *frais* means strawberry." (He pronounced the word "*fraise.*")

There were no fireworks during this close encounter of the second kind. The vegetarian spaghetti we prepared in the kitchen of the hostel made for a pleasant and friendly but unremarkable meal. I remember only that Steve told me he thought Marcel Duchamp's portrait should be on the 100-franc note. (It turned out he was not an archeologist, but an artist, and the deep and even tan came not from a dig, but from the extensive bicycle touring he had done around Europe that summer.) He gave me the phone number of the friends he would be staying with outside Paris, "in case you should happen to pass through Paris." I took the number and put it in my pocket, saying that well, I probably would pass through Paris, but not right away. I had other things to do first.

The next morning I left the hostel early. It was raining again and as I headed down the street toward the train station, the cheap plastic poncho I was wearing became the prop for a Don Quixote-like episode in which I, burdened with my backpack and hampered by my flimsy poncho, clumsily navigated the narrow streets through a fairly heavy rain, during which gusts of wind brought the poncho with regular and maddening frequency over my face, blinding me and causing me to stumble. It was irritating: but the train station wasn't far away, and it was hard to dampen my spirits for very long. I found my way onto the train for Rouen, initiating the use of my thirty-day Eurail pass, and feeling extremely adventurous.

The very first new word I learned in France was, appropriately, the word for "strike." The train pulled out of the station, moved a short distance and then stopped and didn't move for a very long time. "*Pourquoi...*" I finally dared to ask, and the handsome young Frenchman who was sharing a pole with me responded with a rueful grin, "*Grève.*" That was how I learned that French strikes tend to favor slowing down and annoying passengers, rather than totally interrupting service. Accordingly, we did reach our destination that day with no problem, just a bit late.

For me Rouen, the town where Joan of Arc had met her final fate, with its fifteenth century buildings, was a fitting introduction to the Continent. I had always been taken with the story of the simple country girl who had followed her vision and led the rightful King of France to his coronation. I stayed there a day and then, in fulfillment of the plan my American friend in London had helped me devise, went to Bayeux to see the famous tapestry, and spent a wonderful day biking to Arromanches, where I visited the Musée du Débarquement and devoured the details of recent history that (I later learned) had involved some of my own relatives.

Back in Bayeux that night, a Saturday night, I found that *Dr. Zhivago* was playing (dubbed in French, of course), and decided that watching one of my favorite films and hearing it spoken in French was a great opportunity, far more important than taking the time (and having the courage) to eat another meal in a restaurant by myself. The night before, in Rouen, I had eaten alone, ordering with a spirit of adventure, and had regretted my choice. I could eat a big meal tomorrow, I told myself, and get by with popcorn and a chocolate bar for tonight.

So it was that in the following days I nearly suffered the embarrassment of starving to death in France—a country known throughout the world for its fine cuisine—and in the process learned about Sunday nights and Mondays in France, when most if not all of the businesses are closed, and the merchants who have provided for all those leisurely Sunday feasts for their neighbors take a day of rest for themselves.

Essoyes in Champagne

Ours was not a case of love at first sight. It took three rather gross and unsubtle shoves of fate before Steve and I submitted to what began to seem our inevitable joint destiny, went ahead, and fell in love. The first two encounters I have already described: our chance meeting on a ferry on the English Channel, and our unlikely reunion an hour and a half later in a youth hostel in Dieppe, where we shared vegetarian spaghetti and talked about our travels in Europe—his a recent *fait accompli*, mine just beginning.

A few days later, when I arrived in Paris, I took him up on his invitation to look him up "if I should happen to pass through" town. He was living in Bry-sur-Marne, one of the eastern suburbs of Paris: he came into town to meet me, and brought along his friend Chick, who had just arrived from San Francisco. The three of us had a great time together: we went to see a film, and afterward walked around Paris talking about the things young Americans talk about when they are abroad together. Before returning to Bry, where they were staying with French friends, they walked me to my hotel in the Latin Quarter.

They told me they would be leaving Paris the next day for some time, more than a week, and said that perhaps when they returned I would be away on my travels. They were going to pick grapes in the Champagne region. They paused, then asked me if I would I like to go along with them. The vineyard owners seemed to need more workers, they said.

Would I? And why would I not?! The proposal was very attractive to me for a number of reasons, none of them having anything to do with either Steve or Chick, though I liked them both and found being in their company pleasant. But the chance to see the French countryside close up and from the inside? To integrate myself into the culture, the language, to get to know the people? The chance to have free room and board for ten days or so? And to even earn some money on top of that?

I said yes.

With my quick acceptance of their invitation, they looked at each other in puzzled consternation. "Well, ah…" Steve said nervously. "Actually, I don't think there's room in the car we're going in."

"No problem," I said. "Just tell me where to go and I'll meet you there." I had my Eurail pass, I was ready to travel. So they gave me a phone number scrawled on a little piece of paper, and the name of the town closest to the vineyards that had a train station, Bar-sur-Seine. As I write this more than forty years later it occurs to me for the first time in many times of telling this story a bit curious that they even had this much information in their possession that night: they were being conveyed into the countryside by French friends, and knew very little about where they were going or what they would be doing there. But as fate would have it, they did have with them the very tidbits of information I would need to get myself to the *vendange* on time, and they shared them with me. I took the phone number, put it in my pocket, and said I would see them there.

And again, as fate would have it, I got there ahead of them. "What do I say when I call this number?" I had asked Steve and Chick as we stood outside my hotel in Paris that night, and they had said, breezily, "Oh, just tell them you're with Steve and Chick." This had sounded good at the time but it was less than effective when I arrived in Bar-sur-Seine the next day and told the Frenchwoman who ran the train station the same thing. She had offered to make the phone call for me, seeing how limited my ability to speak French was. Mine was the last train of the day to come into the little station, and she was eager to dispense with me, the last passenger, so she could close the station and prepare her family's dinner. "*Steeeev-uh? Cheeek?*" she squeaked, turning Steve's name into two syllables and stretching Chick's out as far as it could go. The person on the other end of the phone, whoever it was, knew nothing about anyone named Steve or Chick. Though I couldn't speak French very well yet, my ability to understand it was better. "Look, I have *une anglaise* here," the Frenchwoman said into the phone, somewhat impatiently. (She thought I was English.) "She wants to pick grapes. Do you want her? If you do, please come and get her, the sooner the better. If not, I don't know what to do with her." Then she hung up the phone and gave me to understand that someone would soon be coming to get me.

A short time later, a shortish, rather stout, but not unattractive Frenchman strode into the station. He had intense, bright, dark brown eyes, bad teeth, a winsome smile, and the stump of a cigar in one corner of his mouth. The stationmaster waved an arm toward me as he entered the station, and the Frenchman held out his hand to me in greeting. As we walked out of the station toward his car, it briefly occurred to me that on principle what I was about to do was not the best idea in the world. I was going to get into a car with a stranger, a man that I knew not at all, and drive off to a place, I knew not where. No one in the world knew where I was, I didn't know where I was going either, and soon it would be dark.

But his eyes were kind, and there was the tenuous chain of connection that led back through Steve and Chick to an unknown French friend of theirs. This was not, therefore, a totally random and careless act, I told myself. A combination of confidence in my intuition and the knowledge that a chain of friendship connected me with the man I was following to the car convinced me to lay aside any hesitation and embrace the adventure before me.

We got into the car, and drove off. As I recall, Jacques (for the man was Jacques Roger, who was to become a close and dear friend), tried to communicate with me, but this was problematic. I spoke very little French; he spoke and understood no English; and his French was difficult for me to understand, especially because of the cigar. So we rode along, mostly in silence. We drove a short distance before he parked the car and began to get out. I too began to unfasten my seat belt, but he grunted and gestured for me to stay where I was. He entered a building and returned a few minutes later. We drove some more, not long this time either, still within the town of Bar-sur-Seine. This time we stopped in front of a modern apartment building, and this time I waited for him to indicate whether I should get out of the car or not. I should. We were *chez lui*.

It was now fully dark. The building we entered was modern, cold and charmless, but we proceeded to a small, simple apartment, full of warmth and light. Jacques's beautiful young wife greeted me, and their toddler daughter, Béthsabée, peeked at me shyly from behind her mother's knees. Josette had prepared a simple but tasty meal, and Jacques brought out a bottle of champagne. As the champagne flowed, we talked. (It was easier for me to understand Josette than Jacques, and she also knew a little bit of English, which she was happy to practice.) But mostly we spoke French, and as the champagne took its effect, my words flowed more easily. For a while I tried to explain who Steve and Chick were, and how I had come to be there, but it was too complicated and after a while it seemed to matter very little. I was there to help pick grapes, perhaps Steve and Chick would arrive to do the same, perhaps not. We began to talk about other things—life, art, American politics. After a while they showed me to their guest room, and wished me a good night.

Just before falling asleep, as my head was sinking gratefully into a sumptuous feather pillow, I heard the phone ring. A few minutes later there was a soft tapping at my door, then Josette poked her head inside. "Your friends have arrived," she whispered in French. "You'll see them in the morning."

Very early the next morning—before dawn—I was awakened with the same soft tapping at my door. Josette had prepared coffee and croissants for me and Jacques, and after a hasty and quiet breakfast, we got back into the car to go the vineyards. It was about a twenty-minute ride, first along a tree-lined national route that led from Bar-sur-Seine to Celles, where we turned off of the *route natio- nale* and took smaller roads through a series of villages. Celles, the first village we passed through, had a huge champagne bottle sculp- ture made of champagne bottles at the entrance to the town, and the names of *caves* and vintners were posted on many of the buildings we passed by. We were in Champagne country!

We arrived in the vineyard where the harvest would begin that day just as a pink dawn was breaking. There was an assortment of workers—old Frenchmen and women, whole families of *manouches* (one of the words for French gypsies), a few French students, and the Parisian entourage of which Steve and Chick were two, and the only Americans. One of the group they had traveled with from Paris was a young Irishwoman, another was a French university student who later caused Jacques and his brother no small amount of con- sternation by staging his own mini-strike for higher wages and attempting—ultimately unsuccessfully—to attract others to his cause. We all stood around ready to begin work, waiting for instruc- tions. Steve and Chick had come over to greet me as we arrived, and explained that their car had broken down, causing their late arrival in Essoyes—the village we were now near—the night before. They were glad to see me, glad I had gotten there safely and found my way to the vines. Shortly afterward Francoise Roger, a no-nonsense Frenchwoman who we later learned was Jacques's sister-in-law, stepped onto an overturned crate and began to assign working units by pointing imperiously at pairs of workers. "*Vous! Vous! Vous!*" she cried. She put me and Steve together, pointed us toward our first vine—and our life as a couple, though we did not know it at that time, had begun.

Steve, seen through the vines, 1978

Learning French

After the *vendange*, at Jacques's invitation we had stayed on for about a week in Essoyes. He had taken a special liking to us: perhaps it was partly because we were the only young, university-type pickers who declined to join the effort by the French students who were threatening to strike. We knew we had a good deal, why would we do that? In any case, Jacques told us we could stay in the house we were lodged in for as long as we wanted, and he and Josette invited us to a Sunday meal in their home that none of us will ever forget. I'm sorry to say that part of the reason for that is that we indulged ourselves actually to the point of physical discomfort. But the food was all SO GOOD!!! And there were so many courses, and there was so much wine that went along with the food…

Then it was time to go our separate ways: Steve went back to Bry-sur-Marne; Chick on to Germany, where his goal was to learn German well enough to read Rilke in the original; and I needed to continue using my Eurail pass, which I used to travel first to Amsterdam, and then on to Spain.

Hours of backbreaking, knee-bending work picking grapes on opposite sides of a vine had created a situation, as Steve put it, in which "you either fall in love with the person across from you, or you come to hate them." We fell in love. And, Paris being situated where it is, it was easy for me to continue with my independent travel and still see Steve once in a while. So my train pass took me to Amsterdam, then back to Paris. To San Sebastian, Madrid, Granada, Sevilla, Madrid; then back to Paris. Like that. Later, for a while I shuttled back and forth between London and Paris, because through a fluke I had been able to find work typing in London for a temp agency, and I was lucky enough to be able to stay with the friend of a friend who was studying there.

When I had first gone to Europe one of my goals had been to choose between France and Spain: which place did I want to return to, to stay as long as I could (somehow), and become truly fluent in the language? At the time, my Spanish was better than my French. I had studied it more recently and was more skilled in it because I had practiced it during my first international trip, to Mexico.

Then I met Steve, and he was living in France. Though I knew that Spanish was probably a more *practical* language to learn, especially for a citizen of the US, and that although Spanish too is a very beautiful language with a rich body of literature, learning French began to seem more the thing to do. (The fiction that I was at least *trying* to be a practical person was beginning to be exposed. So was the fact that I was falling in love.)

But how to do it. Though we enjoyed the time we spent together, Steve needed time alone more than he needed time with me, that was obvious. I was welcome for visits, sometimes fairly long visits, and he always seemed sad when I left, but he didn't want me living with him.

Surprisingly, my typing skill had even come in handy while I was in Europe. When I had first arrived in London, and was asked by the Customs and Border Patrol people how long I intended to stay, I told the truth: a week. They stamped my passport, added no particular restrictions, and that is why later, I was able to work there as a "temp." I had assumed I would not be able to work in England, not being a citizen of the Common Market, but when I went back there several months later to visit the friend of a friend (who was by now becoming a friend), as I walked around London I saw so many sandwich boards outside of temp agencies calling for typists, that one day I thought, well what can it hurt to ask? I'll go in, they'll hear my accent, they'll throw me out, and that will be that.

But that is not what happened. They asked to see my passport, I showed them my passport, and to my great surprise they sent me out on my first assignment, to Ruck & Ruck, a property management company. That assignment didn't last long: that is the place where I made the mistake—in working from a Dictaphone—of spelling Berkeley Square the way it sounded to me: Barkley Square. There was a horrified squeal of disbelief from my supervisor as I handed him my first typed letter. "Barkley Square!! We'll be the laughing stock of London!" he sputtered before telling me this wasn't going to work out. So I went back to the agency, and again to my surprise, they sent me out again. I learned to ask more questions, even about things I thought I knew (that was a delicate task!) and, with a more understanding and forgiving next boss, it was fine.

Finally, in February, when my money was about to run out, I returned to Minneapolis. I had been in Europe for five months. I was now determined to find a way back to France as soon as I could. A way that would allow me to be there without having to live with Steve.

Of course there was the possibility of a return to school, graduate studies in French, a study abroad program. But none of these would have solved my problem in the least. I wanted to go back to France more or less *now*. And not for a defined, restricted, and highly structured period of time.

* * *

The way back came. I believe it always *does* come if you are determined enough, and if you are willing to ignore all the imperfections of the particular way that opens up before you. In this case it came thanks to friends of friends in Minneapolis who knew of a retreat center in the south of France run by Protestant nuns—yes, Protestant nuns.

There was just one little catch, in terms of my ostensible main reason for returning to France: the retreat center run by the Protestant nuns in the south of France was "a place of silence." And since my supposed main purpose in returning to France was to learn French, how was this going to work? But the nuns accepted *stagiaires,* people who could stay there for free, and work in return for room and board. And I could go there right away, or as soon as I had earned enough money to pay for my ticket and some money to spare. "They have to speak *sometimes,*" I reasoned, and decided that the problem of the silent nature of the place was a detail I would worry about later. So, after saving up enough spending money to last me for at least a few months by working more typing jobs at the University of Minnesota, I returned to France. I flew to Paris and stayed for a little while with Steve, and then it was on to Provence, to the tiny village of Saint-Etienne-du-Grès, near Tarascon. To Pomeyrol, the rural retreat center, the "place of silence" run by Protestant nuns, who wore brown robes, not black ones.

I was assigned to work with a pretty, kind young Swedish sister who spoke English, but—understanding without really being told the main purpose of my being there—she spoke to me in French. She was in charge of housekeeping. So I made beds and cleaned toilets and scrubbed floors, and along the way I learned useful vocabulary—the words for pillows (various kinds), sheets, broom and mop, pail and brush. (All words that are *not* cognates in English, by the way. Most of the words that you can guess, in going from English to French, are more useful in intellectual discussions. Abstract words like nation and revolution, didactic, ephemeral.) While I was there, I also learned a lot of words used in religious settings. There were more cognates in this category than in the housekeeping category, but not that many. Most of those words were new too. (*Louange. Bénissement. Miséricorde.*) I learned how deep the meaning of concepts like numbers are when I tried to play a duet in chapel one day with another flutist. I made the mistake of beginning my (silent) count in French. And when the composition became complicated and our parts diverged rhythmically, I learned that the words "*un deux trois quatre*" had absolutely no deep meaning for me. I was completely lost and I stumbled until I could pick up the (silent) count again, in English.

I was there for—how long, I don't know—maybe six weeks, maybe two months? I had arrived there in June or July, and by September I was back with Steve, in Bry-sur-Marne, about sixteen kilometers east of Paris. By now he had purchased *la roulotte*, which would be his home for the next couple of years, and whenever I stayed with him, it was mine too.

La roulotte was a classic, antique gypsy caravan, made in 1938 for one Madame Nouvelle, whose name and the letters SDF (for *sans domicile fixe)* were engraved into the chassis. "She," that is *la roulotte,* was sitting in the garden of our friend Jean-Lou's home in Bry-sur-Marne, just across a small road along the banks of the Marne River, not far from a kayak club and the bridge over the river into Le Perreux. At the top of a steep hill that took up most of the garden, facing Avenue du Général LeClerc, was Jean-Lou's house, where he lived with an odd assortment of *marginal* friends, coworkers, hangers-on, and outright abusers of his generosity. While we were living there Jean-Lou became involved with a woman who attempted to impose domesticity and a greater degree of sanity on the place. She cleaned and painted and got some of the worst abusers of Jean-Lou's generosity to leave. She had brought with her a four-year-old daughter, and then she and Jean-Lou had a child together. For a while things were indeed a bit more sane, and a lot cleaner. She did not stay forever, but she stayed longer than we did.

By now I was more or less living with Steve. I had gotten work in the mornings selling pots and pans in the marketplaces around Paris and the surrounding suburbs with his friend Colette, and in the afternoons I was taking classes at the Alliance Francaise. Steve was taking advantage of the generosity of the Institut des Beaux Arts, which at the time offered artists the opportunity to draw from the model at no charge. And Chick was still living in Germany, working in taverns and happily reading Rilke.

It was at the Alliance Francaise that I met my friend Istvan, a young Hungarian about my age who had escaped from what was still then behind the "Iron Curtain." He was the one who introduced himself to me. Whether because of his personality, his limited English, or his strong desire to become acquainted with Americans, he simply approached me one day after class, and said, "Are you American?" and when I said that I was, he asked, "Would you have coffee with me?" We went together to a café where he began asking me questions, eager to know about the nature of life in places that it had been forbidden for him to know about. One day he said, in a tone of awe and disbelief, "I have heard that in New York **every day** there is **one murder**." "One?!" I replied. "There's *gotta* be more than that..." Which led of course to a discussion about guns in the US. He couldn't understand why we had so many guns, why just about any-one could be carrying one. I tried to explain about the Second Amendment, and the belief of many Americans that the right to carry weapons was an important kind of freedom. "But isn't it a kind of freedom to walk around safely without being shot at?" he asked. "Well, yes," I said. "Many of us feel that way. In any case," I assured him, "most of the people shooting each other know each other. So it's to a large degree a question of staying on good terms with the people you know."

Somehow he didn't seem to find that so assuring. And sadly, at this writing it's no longer true what I told him back then. It's no longer enough to stay on good terms with the people you know. Not in 2022. Not in the United States.

A Cheap Loft in the West Village

Now my shuttles grew longer: greater distances, longer lengths of time. Paris-Minneapolis-New York-Paris-New York-Paris. Eventually, there were hard decisions to be made. Where was I going to live? Who was I going to build the rest of my life with? And was I going to be able to avoid heartbreak, my own or someone else's?

It was during this period of time, which lasted a couple of years, that Steve, Chick, and I were together once again in Paris in the summer of 1980.

Chick had come from Germany for a visit, and as we were wandering the streets of Paris one night, talking about what we should do next, we had all agreed it was time to go home. For me the romance of selling pots and pans in the marketplace was wearing thin, as was the necessity of hiding from the *gendarmes* whenever they came around to check papers. I was also reaching the end of my patience with various annoying aspects of dealing with life in France. For example, in those days before email and cell phones, it was necessary to deal with the French postal service in order to communicate "across the pond" either by phone, or by what we now call snail mail. And that could be aggravating. Aggravation in one's own home is one thing, and aggravation abroad is quite another: the latter tends to make you feel like tossing your head, huffing off, and going home where people are more "reasonable."

In any case, we had all come to feel, each of us for slightly different reasons, that if we wanted to take the next step in our lives, whatever that was, it was time for a change. And that is how we came to be discussing the how, when, and where that night. All that remained was to do it.

This is the context in which the tale of the Cheap Loft in the West Village was created. I realized long ago that I will never live down having "promised" Steve and Chick, in that summer of 1980, that we could quite easily find a loft to rent in the West Village for about $50 a month. Actually, I did not say anything of the kind, though neither did I work very hard to dissuade them of the notion that finding a place to live in New York City was a perfectly reasonable venture. In fact, I very distinctly remember avoiding eye contact with Chick as I answered his question, "But hasn't it gotten awfully expensive to live in New York?"

"I think it's the kind of thing where, if you really want to do it, you can find a way," I said, elliptically. I had just stated in no uncertain terms, that if we were going to return to the States, there really was only one place worth living, and that was New York City. I didn't want to back off of this statement, which I felt to be both completely true and extremely important. Thus began the Myth of the $50 Loft in the West Village.

The first time the tale was told, I think they said that I had promised them something in the neighborhood of $200 a month. But it made a better story for my claim to be even more outrageous, and so the price worked its way down the ladder until it arrived at $50, where it has remained ever since. I never tried very hard to stamp out the myth. Why would I? What a good story it made, and how it has amused our friends through the years!

And so we all decided it was time for us to go back home, to the US. But what to do with *la roulotte*, now that was the question.

Jacques came to the rescue, offered to keep it in Essoyes, next to the building where his tractors were stored. It would be safe there, and he asked for no rent. Steve hired a flatbed truck to haul the *roulotte* from the banks of the Marne outside of Paris to Champagne. And soon after we were on our way, to New York City.

Proceeding with our bold plan, Steve and I preceded Chick by a few weeks, with the plan of finding a place for the three of us to live in New York.

It was not a smooth landing. New York City in August is hot. Anyone who is able to get out of there in August does so: and that is when we arrived there, ready to create our future.

And the weather wasn't our only problem: we had very little money, we had no jobs, and the only person we knew in New York was my ex-boyfriend, who was not very happy with me at the time.

The first night we got a room in the Chelsea Hotel: but even though it was funky, definitely a down-at-the-heels atmosphere, it was not cheap, and we knew we couldn't stay there for long. After one night there we found other lodgings in an even funkier hotel off of Lexington Avenue in the East 50s. I don't remember what we paid, but I do remember we figured out that our money could stretch there for only about a week, during which time we needed to find a place to live. It was a dreadful place: there was no air conditioning and our room was infested with cockroaches that would scurry, *en masse*, from wherever they were, *including the bed*, when we entered the room and turned on the light. The concierge was a bug-eyed woman whose thick glasses made her more so: she wore harsh, caked-on makeup and had straw-like, bleached blonde hair with dark roots: her name was Mrs. Lyons, and she was indeed pretty fierce.

We started scouring the papers, mostly the *Village Voice*, and looking at places. It was hard to find anything we could even try for: we had about $1,000 and the lowest rent we could find was around $400 a month. With the security deposit, and the first and last month's rent required up front, that was more than we had.

E.B. White wrote, in his wonderful essay, "Here is New York" that "no one should come to New York planning to live there if he is not willing to be lucky." We got lucky. We found a place—it was a corner bedroom within a newly renovated loft on West 38th Street, in the garment district—for $400 a month. By the time we got there, there was already a long list of interested prospective tenants: but for some reason, the twenty-something owner/landlord who would in effect become our roommate, chose us. He took $800, and waived the security deposit—or was it the last month's rent?—which meant that we had a cool $200 left, and now we had a place to live.

We moved in right away, an easy move since all we had with us at that time could fit into our backpacks. Steve bought lumber and built us a loft bed, and he found a rocking chair at a moving sale. He brought it home on his bicycle by strapping the chair onto his back, creating a sight that was given the greatest form of recognition any New Yorker can receive: as he rode down Ninth Avenue, he overheard someone say, "I've lived in New York a long time, and I've seen a lotta things, but I've never seen that!" with an appreciative laugh.

Now we needed jobs. During the time I had been shuttling back and forth between New York and Paris, I had worked for what was then called Kelly Girls as a typist, and again I found myself in some very interesting situations. One job had involved wrapping commemorative "Big Apples" made of Steuben glass, for the inaugural event at a newly opening hotel. Another offered me the curious sight of an unmade bed in a bedroom just off the office in a—was it a law firm? I don't remember. What was a bed doing in the office? I wondered. I didn't know but it certainly provided interesting possibilities to consider, and raised my protective instincts as well.

In almost every single place I worked during this period, after a day or two I would be called into the office of my supervisor, who would offer me permanent employment. I always declined. Because now I wanted to go *back* to Europe. The other thing I remember is how inevitably, in the first couple of days I was on the job someone, sometimes more than one someone, would confide to me conspiratorially, about how this office was "really crazy." The conclusion I drew, and one that has not changed, is that office environments are all pretty crazy, as was later dramatized in the television series, *The Office.*

When many years later I managed to land a full-time, though temporary, contract position as a writer in a federal agency in Washington, I remember the feeling I had when I first sat at my assigned desk in an office with stale air, no natural light, my desk facing a wall, and contemplated how many hours were left in that first day. It was the feeling I imagined a wild animal would have if caught in a trap. It was all I could do to suppress a howl. And yet, that job provided "sustenance," and I worked there for more than a year. My colleagues were nice, the mission was a good one, and that made it bearable, but it was always a struggle for me and I probably couldn't have stayed as long as I did if I hadn't been able to do most of my work from my laptop, sitting in the library, where I was able to look out a window, where I could see trees, and sky, and grass. And of course I was very grateful if not for the actual work, at least for the "pellets" they gave me in that cage.

* * *

That first fall in New York I had learned that they were recruiting typists for the English language typing pool at the United Nations. So I went through their battery of tests, and I was hired. I remember the supercilious attitude of the handsome young South American bureaucrat who administered the test. He wore tight pants, cowboy boots, and an apparently permanent sneer on his face: I imagined that he led a double life, the other half being lived in one of the S/M bars—the Spike, or the Anvil, or the Nail—in the meat-packing district just west of the West Village. He strode around the room where we were being tested making snide and condescending remarks: the only thing lacking was a whip.

By this time Chick had arrived from Europe and had installed himself in our closet, which we were also using as a darkroom. (In one of my last attempts to avoid focusing on my real talent in life, for a while I had aspirations of becoming a photographer. I had a good eye, but that was all. It wasn't enough!)

So we had found our perch in Manhattan, but it was not exactly comfortable. Our bedroom had a sliding glass door with a curtain that closed it off from the main part of the sunny loft, which meant you had to choose between light and privacy: you couldn't have both at the same time. Theoretically we were sharing the open communal living space, but since the other couple's bed was more or less in the middle of that space, it didn't really feel communal. It felt like their loft, which it was, and most of the space was dominated by our land-lord/roommate, a talented former semi-pro athlete and current jazz singer who was spending most of his time sitting around watching television, drinking beer, snorting cocaine, and eating one baked potato a day.

I had the job at the UN: now Steve and Chick needed jobs too. They had both made money sanding floors in San Francisco, but they really didn't want to do that again if they could find something else to do. I remembered that an acquaintance of my ex-boyfriend did contracting work, fixing up old houses somewhere in the city. Maybe he could give them some work.

Frank was an alternate-side-of-the-street acquaintance. In New York, on-the-street parking is so competitive that you can't just move your car from one side of the street to the other at the time appointed for street cleaning: if you wait until then, all the spaces are taken up. So you have to move the car about an hour ahead of time, and then sit in it, to prevent it from being ticketed or towed, and wait until it's legal to leave it there. Sitting in, or leaning against their cars a couple of times a week, Frank and my boyfriend had struck up a casual acquaintance.

On the basis of that casual acquaintance, which was even more casual for me—I had only met Frank once or twice—I urged Steve and Chick to call him and see if he had any work for them. They called him from a phone booth, and he told them to come out to Brooklyn, he might have some work for them. They met him in Ft. Greene, where he was involved in restoring beautiful 19th-century brownstones that had fallen into disrepair, bringing them back to their former glory.

The first job he gave them was to sheetrock a room. That job could have gone better.

Frank was a wonderful human being, and he became a good friend: but he occasionally lacked patience for the learning curve of others. In this case, when he returned after a couple of days to check on Steve and Chick's progress, he entered the room, looked around, stepped back, and offered them one of those pricelessly charged reactions—all exaggerated body language and infinitely nuanced facial expression—that New Yorkers are so good at. Then he said, with perfect timing, hands turned up in a gesture of incredulousness, voice squeaking in disbelief, "Two men? Two days?!"

However, he did not fire them. He gave them more work, and they became part of a team of workers that included the man who was to provide us with our first home in Brooklyn, in the unfinished attic of a brownstone with a beautiful view of Ft. Greene Park—and from our rooftop, a view of the city beyond. And for a long time, we lived there rent-free.

On the Brooklyn Bridge, c. 1983

Ft. Greene, Brooklyn

It was February of 1981 when we moved into that unfinished attic. One of Steve and Chick's coworkers on the brownstone renovation projects they'd been working on with Frank felt sorry for us for some reason, and he offered us a place to live for free, for some undetermined length of time.

We had lasted only six months in Manhattan, and I cried when we had to leave. "But it's so pretty in Brooklyn!" Steve said, "There are trees there..." "I don't want trees, I want the *New York Times* and the diner downstairs," I protested. But there was no way we could afford Manhattan, that was obvious.

Our new landlord—well, really at the time, he was just a friend giving us a place to stay—picked us up at the loft on West 38th Street and drove us in his van to our new home. We trudged up the stairs to the top floor—formerly a ballroom, we were told—and looked around for places to put our meager belongings. All we had was our backpacks, the loft bed Steve had made, a chest of drawers we had taken in from the sidewalk, several boxes of books and clothes, Steve's drawing table, and the rocking chair he had bicycled home with a few months earlier. But the attic was a classic "Noah's ark" stuffed full of the owner's odd assortment of possessions ("Two of everything!" Steve joked). That first night we managed to find room for our mattress, the only new thing we owned, and we left the other things in the hallways.

Over the months that followed we gradually carved out more space for ourselves, and the owner gradually, bit by bit, took his things away, to a country home he had purchased in upstate New York. If there was a piece of furniture we were particularly fond of we would try to keep it out of his notice by keeping it covered with clothing or blankets, so we wouldn't lose it. "Oh!" he would say, with an air of discovery. "That's nice! I should take that upstate..." and there would go one of our favorite places to sit.

One half of the former ballroom had finished walls at least, but the other half was open beams, there was no ceiling or walls, and there were leaks in the roof. We got to know where they all were, and when it would rain we had buckets ready to catch the water. There was no kitchen—what little "cooking" we did we did in a toaster oven. There was a toilet, and a bathtub with a showerhead, but there were no doors, except the one leading from the front half to the back half of the floor: we used the cardboard carton that the tub had come in as a handy portable "screen" for privacy when using the toilet. There was a hole in the floor between the two halves of the place that *we* were used to stepping over, but my sister was not, and on one of her visits she went plunging into the hole with a comical yowl. (Fortunately she was not hurt, and true to family tradition she took it in stride.)

It was, in a word, "rustic." It was a classic garret. But it was what we could afford (nothing); it was home, and we lived there for twelve years. Then we moved into an apartment in a brownstone a few houses down the block from the first one for another two years.

Our new home was on a block of beautiful 19th century brownstones, right across from Ft. Greene Park, which had been designed by Olmsted and Vaux, the same team that had created Central Park in Manhattan, and Prospect Park in Brooklyn. Though it was dangerous to walk in at night, it was beautiful during the day. The park is on the site of a fort that had been important during the Battle of Brooklyn in the Revolutionary War. On the crest of the hill overlooking the housing project on the north side of the park, a monument to the more than 11,000 prison ship "martyrs" who had died on British ships in Wallabout Bay—a 148-foot Doric column designed by McKim, Mead and White—was dedicated in 1908.

Their bones, which had begun to wash up on the shore in the years following the war, are in a crypt beneath the monument.

On holiday weekends in the summers, especially Memorial Day and Labor Day, and of course the Fourth of July, the park filled with families that came from neighborhoods that didn't have such lovely parks; they set up their lawn chairs and tables, their picnics and barbecues. All day long the music would play, and often there was even a live mariachi band adding to the festive atmosphere. It was no day to get any work done, except cleaning the house, which I often did on those days. But it was always pleasant to be in the midst of all that joy, and a good way to make housecleaning bearable, with lively Latin music coming in through our open windows.

For the first few years we lived there, there was a handsome elderly gentleman named Sal who either worked for the city or simply cared a lot about that park. Especially on mornings after nights when there had been partying in the park we would hear him raking the sidewalk adjacent to the park early in the morning, patiently cleaning up the debris. It was a lovely sound to wake up to, suggesting that after chaos, even joyful chaos, there would again be order.

Stoop sitting was a regular part of life there, and although that is not exactly how we came to be friends with our next-door neighbors (that had more to do with the fact that we both had dogs), we developed a habit of entering their home not the normal way, by ringing the doorbell and going into the building through the front door, but by shouting out to them from their stoop, and entering their apartment through their parlor-level windows.

Spike Lee was one of our neighbors, and he became famous during the time we lived there. He lived in a rented ground-floor apartment in one of the brownstones on the block, about halfway between our first home and our second one. By the time we moved out of the neighborhood, to Flatbush, he had become successful enough to buy his own brownstone on the end of the block.

I happened to witness a scene between Spike and some of the neighborhood kids one day. Three young boys—they looked to be about twelve, I guess, one of them maybe a bit younger—were hanging around across the street from his place. I don't remember if they screwed up the nerve to call out to him, or if he just happened to see them there when he came outside. In any case, he started a conversation with them from across the street. They asked for his autograph, and he invited them to approach. "How many you need?" he asked them as the two older boys started to cross the street. They looked at each other, as if calculating just how lucky they were going to be, and then one of them said, "Two." Spike cocked his head a bit, paused, and then said, "I think you really need three don't you?" The older boys nodded sheepishly, and the younger boy, who was hanging back, smiled a sweet smile. I couldn't hear the rest of what passed between them; but I was impressed with that scene.

One of the biggest advantages of living on the top floor of the first brownstone we lived in was our access to the roof, which we could reach by climbing up a fire escape ladder at the top of our stairs, and opening a hatch. It wasn't legal to do so, but we had lots of wonderful barbecues up there, using our little Weber grill, a big bucket of water and fire extinguisher always at the ready. There was a beautiful view from there looking over the park, especially at sunset, the Williamsburg Savings Bank with its clock tower a comforting beacon in one direction, and the glittering lights of Manhattan in the other. It was a great place to watch the fireworks on the Fourth of July. One particularly memorable Fourth we pulled our phone up through the hatch with a long extension phone cord, because Chick and his wife were expecting their first child any day, and we had offered to drive them to the hospital if they needed a ride when the time came. It turned out that the time came at exactly the moment when it was impossible to get a cab, as everyone was leaving the Brooklyn Heights Promenade after watching the fireworks. The phone rang on our rooftop, I heard Steve say, "So what you're saying is..." We rushed off, and got them to the hospital in time.

When we moved out of Ft. Greene in 1995, further into Brooklyn, I cried again as we were walking through the park one day on our way to the subway. It was another February day, and our move was imminent. "How can you cry about leaving this place?" Steve asked. He was alluding to the high rate of crime in the neighborhood, which was the main thing fueling our move.

Of course I didn't mind moving to a less crime-ridden neighborhood, but I did mind leaving the trees, and those beautiful brownstones, behind.

Embracing the Dream

Those first few years in New York City were pretty exciting. Steve is a very talented artist, and he was determined to make his mark in the New York art world. That is, in one way he was. In another way, he was always more interested in making his art than in making his mark in the art world, and artists tend to have to pay for that kind of idealism.

After not getting fired by Frank on their first job, he and Chick continued to work with him part-time as handymen, and the rest of the time Steve was free to do his work. We didn't have much money, but we didn't need much. We were paying no rent, and the rest of our needs were modest. Steve was studying at the Art Students League, determined to learn what he had not learned at the Rhode Island School of Design during the height of the "conceptual art" movement: now he was focusing on figure drawing and studying human anatomy.

We spent a fair amount of what income we had eating at Cino's, the local Italian restaurant on DeKalb Avenue, where we became regulars, primarily because the attic we were living in didn't have a kitchen; initially we had just a hotplate and a butane burner, and later a toaster oven. So it wasn't very conducive to preparing home-cooked meals, especially for two not very impressive cooks with other things on their mind. Later, when I was in graduate school, my parents bought us a microwave oven and that helped, a lot. And a bit after that, a room opened up on the second floor of the building, and we took it over. That room had a gas stove and an oven, so we were able to cook real meals.

My typing job at the UN had only lasted a few months. Every fall before the General Assembly sessions began, they would hire a cadre of typists, and each year keep the cream of the crop. It was a plum job if you didn't mind the tedium of typing your life away, but I didn't have to decide whether I wanted to stay there. The year I was hired was the same year they were switching from IBM Selectric typewriters to a word-processing machine called Wang. That year, anticipating greater efficiency through word processing, they knew they didn't need any new typists to stay on, so after the General Assembly session we were all let go, in December.

It was just as well. Though the pay was good, the atmosphere there was rotten. "If the future of world peace and harmony depends on this place…" I muttered more than once in the three months I worked there. There were very demanding "production standards" to meet that made even a very fast and accurate typist like myself afraid to take the time to go to the bathroom. The hiring standards were extremely high, so the typing pool consisted of a lot of very intelligent mostly women, who were also extremely bored, and tired of being treated with disdain and contempt by their supervisors. It was not a happy environment.

So, when the work at the UN was over, I did several more temp assignments through Kelly Girls, and after a few months found my way into a part-time clerical position in the Office of the Dean of Humanities and the Arts at Hunter College. And there I stayed for the next sixteen years, during which time I studied French, English, and American literature, and got my master's degree.

That was a great place to work. The people were nice, the work was interesting, and though the pay wasn't particularly good, it wasn't that bad either. Because it was a union job, even though it was only part-time it had generous benefits, including health insurance. The crew in the Dean's office was typically New York-diverse: my working companions were a middle-aged Jewish mother (divorced); a young Jewish about-to-be-mother who was a niece of Zero Mostel; a talented African-American lesbian poet from somewhere in the South; an elegant young African-American woman who was the daughter of a former US Ambassador to Sweden, who had attended finishing school in Switzerland; a first generation Greek-American graduate student in theater; and a tomboyish, jeans-wearing research assistant from Vermont. The Dean, a Latinist, was also from the South: he had a classic southern drawl, a rather arrogant attitude, and a drinking problem. There was a perhaps natural antipathy between him and the African-American poet from the South; other than that, everyone in this motley crew got along well and we all amused each other. I was particularly amusing to my colleagues, being from Minnesota where we called soda "pop," and believed it was possible for there to be honest politicians. (A belief I expressed one day, which was greeted by an incredulous round of laughter by my colleagues.)

Along with the main crew, there were other equally interesting characters. There was the young adjunct in the Russian Department who taught me how to say *Zdravstvuite*; the Shakespearean scholar who hired me to type the manuscript of an interdisciplinary textbook on the arts he was writing; the fastidious music professor who couldn't stand the smell of smoke, and the heavily made-up, chain-smoking former chair of the theater department who shared an office (and even a desk!) with him. There wasn't a dull character in the bunch.

It was the perfect time and place for me to now do what perhaps I should have done in the first place, which was to study literature. The most obvious and logical thing for me to study when I first went off to college would have been either French or English. But, given the background I was coming from I had naively assumed that if I were to study English, that would lead to one of two career paths—either teaching high-school English in a Minneapolis suburb much like the one I was very ready to get away from (it's surprising in retrospect to think how little imagination I had at that time, at least about *where* I could end up teaching)—or journalism. One of those options seemed too boring to me, the other too scary. Plus, having come from a cultural background where privacy and discretion are two of the strongest, most respected values, and being basically a rather shy person, I wasn't really suited to following a journalistic path.

I knew I had to be practical, at least to some degree. Unlike many of my friends, I had never been encouraged to think that my primary goal in life—or at college—was to find a suitable, breadwinning husband. With the example of my working mom before me, I knew that the problem of how to earn a living was, or at least might very well be, on my own shoulders. And in fact my mother had not only *not* pushed marriage particularly, she told me more than once that a single woman could live a happy, fulfilled life too, and she usually cited several of her friends as examples. This was fairly unusual, and even quite progressive for a woman of her generation.

So I had ended up studying Child Psychology, which was the "practical" subject that was of the most interest to me at the time I was about to drop out of school for the third time. (I was dissuaded by my boyfriend, who, unbeknownst to me at the time, was a college dropout himself. "Don't quit," he said. "But I don't know what I'm *doing!*" I protested. "It doesn't matter," he said. "Just get the degree. You need the degree." "But in what?!" I said. "Anything," he said. "Anything you like." "Okay, Child Psychology!" I said, and he said, "Beautiful. Do it!")

It's the best career advice I've ever had from anyone.

Anyway, now, several years later, here I was, working at a college in the heart of Manhattan, and I could go to school for free, and study anything I wanted! I didn't care about being practical anymore. So of course I wanted to study literature, and I did.

I had to start from scratch. I had read hardly any of the classics, so before taking any graduate classes I filled in the gaps in my reading with undergraduate ones: for example, Backgrounds of Western Literature (the only thing I had read was the Bible, and not very much of that, just the same small parts of it over and over). So now I read Homer, and Virgil, and Dante. And the Book of Job. I took a class in James Joyce's *Ulysses*, and we led up to it with *Dubliners* and *Portrait of the Artist as a Young Man*. I took a class in Chaucer, and I studied 18th century French literature too: Corneille and Racine and Bossuet and Rousseau. I was in heaven!

When I first started studying literature, I thought it was because it would help me learn how to write. One of things that has stayed with me from graduate school was the moment when our professor in a class on literary analysis, Frank Brady, a Boswell scholar, announced at the beginning of the semester that he intended to teach us how to read. I thought I already knew how to do that. But indeed, he taught us a *lot* about how to read. And all of it was, of course, very good training for becoming a better writer.

There had never been any doubt in my mind that I was a writer; I had been a writer from the time I learned to use a pencil, if not before. I just didn't dare to believe I'd ever be able to make my living that way. Now, I suppose, is when it all began to come together. In New York I found what I think all, or at least most writers—and readers too—really long for. Kindred souls: others who love reading and writing as much as you do. In New York they were everywhere. In the subways people were all reading, more then than now, since this was before the days when everyone had their own personal portable entertainment centers offering another way to pass the time by listening to music, or watching videos. In the streets, there was the occasional person strolling while reading a book. But the main thing is that everywhere in the streets of New York were stories—stories being told to friends, neighbors, strangers. Untold stories unfolding before your very eyes, pieces of stories that piqued your curiosity at every turn. And excellent eavesdropping opportunities everywhere. (A regular column in the *New York Times* gave New Yorkers the chance to share choice bits of overheard dialogue with each other. I loved that column; it was called the Metropolitan Diary.)

There were interesting characters everywhere, too. New York characters, brimming with lively dialogue, with ready quips, with homespun wisdom and wisecracks. Even the tabloids had mastered the art of compelling narrative, their headlines jumping out from their places in the newsstand stacks, or hiding the faces of the New Yorkers who were consuming their constant barrage of dramatic tales, inviting smiles, shivers of horror, or curious speculation from those who saw only the headlines. ("Headless Body In Topless Bar" was one of the more memorable, if gruesome, headlines, in the *New York Post.)*

It wasn't all good. One thing I encountered for the first time in New York—not that it doesn't exist elsewhere—was the intense competition that can exist among writers, and especially among would-be writers. In New York I wrote my first essay—it was about some of the psychological/emotional effects that I felt accompanied the change from analog clock faces to digital displays—and in response to that essay I received my first brutal, and cavalierly cruel, criticism. I had entrusted that first brave effort into the world of essay writing to a talented young poet I knew through friends, who was in the MFA program at Columbia. He failed to address in any way the content of my piece, and commented only on its style. "You have no business using this diction," he said dismissively, as he handed it back to me, with circles drawn around the offending words.

I didn't even know what the word "diction" meant in this context at that time—it wasn't a word that had come up in studying Child Psychology—but there was no mistaking the condescension in his voice. My high school *had* prepared me, and my classmates, for the lives the curriculum planners assumed most of us would have: in high school I had learned how to drive; how to type; and how to do my taxes, which I was able to do for myself until I married an artist and doing so became much more complicated. It was a good general education for most of my classmates, and very useful for me as well. But the college prep "track" I was on, though well-meaning, was not nearly as effective. When it came time for me to write my first paper for my freshman English class in college, I was really at a loss. But with the help of an understanding teacher, I had caught up soon enough.

The young poet's criticism of my essay was not only cavalierly cruel: it was also unjustified and off-point. Possibly he was passing on a kind of criticism that he himself had encountered while earning his degree at a pricey private liberal arts college. Though I will never forget the insult, nor regain the respect for him that I lost that day, eventually I was able to understand and forgive, somewhat.

But at the time all I could do was tell myself that I was never going to show my work to *this* person again. And I certainly wasn't going to ask *him* what "diction" meant.

That same essay drew helpful criticism from an older, less competitive, and more generous writer than the one who had disdained it, and helped me get into a writing workshop with Anatole Broyard at the 92nd Street Y. There I learned about the sometimes ungenerous dynamic of the workshop, in which unfortunately many would-be writers are much more eager to tell you whether or not they care about what you have to say, than to listen to what you do have to say and allow it to affect them. Or to give actual, substantive, constructive criticism.

All of it was good for me. The brutal criticism. The helpful criticism. The being in a world where writing mattered enough for people to be either brutal or helpful. The developing of a thick skin, and learning how to know when the criticism was helpful and when it was not.

Of course my dream was really twofold. It wasn't going to be enough for me to be a "real" writer, assuming I could manage to do that (it still seemed a pretty remote possibility to me at that time). I had always wanted also to be a mother. From the time I was in my early twenties and I fell in love with my best friend's young children, I knew I wanted this. I didn't want to do it on my own: for that I needed a partner. It was common among my peers in those early-ish days of "women's lib" to proclaim disinterest in having a family throughout one's twenties, and then to change your mind when the realities of the biological clock set in. I never did that. I knew, always, that I wanted to have children. If I had had to choose between writing and having children, I would have chosen the latter. Eventually this would become a more pressing issue, but for now it was just something I knew was important to me.

* * *

Meanwhile, Steve was doing well with his work: within the first two years of our being in New York he had begun to sell his drawings to museums and private collectors. This came about because he had been to the dentist one day and had gotten a very sobering report of some work he needed to have done. (The sobering part was the cost of it.) "What am I going to do?" he asked me over the phone. "I don't know, we'll figure out something," I said, an early rendition of a phrase that later turned out to be a more or less constant refrain.

When I got home that night, he reported that he had an appointment to show his drawings to the curator of 20th century art at the Metropolitan Museum of Art. "How did you do that?" I said. "I don't know. I just told them I needed an appointment, and they gave me one." The curator was impressed with his work, and bought one of his drawings, leading us to the hasty conclusion that our hard times were over. ("Not dead yet, and in the Met!" he crowed). This turned out to be not true at all, but it was pretty exciting at the time, and it was also a point of pride to learn that this was only the second time in the history of the museum (or perhaps of the department?) that a work had been sold directly to the museum by the artist. Shortly afterward he sold two drawings to the Brooklyn Museum, and several others to private collectors.

After a few years he found a studio space to work in a few blocks away from our home, and there he was able to begin making sculpture. The space was anything but ideal, and his relationship with the landlady was touchy. He may have been one of the few tenants who ever paid their rent. Perhaps that is why she asked him around the first of every month, "Steve, were you going to pay the rent?" a question which, though perfectly reasonable, he found very annoying especially since she had a gratingly nasal, whiny voice.

Eventually he found a great space to work in in the Brooklyn Navy Yard, where among his other neighbors was a company that did set design for *Saturday Night Live*. They struck up a casual friendship when they discovered Steve digging through their very interesting garbage one morning, and after that they would pluck out items they thought he might appreciate, and leave them at the door of his studio. Among the gifts they left were dining room chairs for coneheads, and a catapult. Once they left him some oversized plaster-of-paris angel's wings, which he lived with for a few days and then decided he didn't really want them. So he returned the wings, leaving them with a note that said, "Thanks, guys, but **HE** wouldn't let me in."

We had great parties in that space, and watched many wonderful sunsets over the East River, picnicking and looking toward Manhattan. And we had a great view of the fireworks from there every Fourth of July. It was in that studio that Steve once constructed an 18-foot model of a Tyrannosaurus Rex bound for an exhibition in Japan, one of *his* oddest jobs ever. And it is there also that he built a beautiful series of sculptures—etched glass and steel, mostly— exploring the nexus of science, art, and religion, culminating in his masterpiece, "The Standard Model (abandoned)," a 40-foot-long sculptural interpretation of a particle accelerator. That piece landed him his first one-man show at a gallery in Soho, and was also exhibited at Brookhaven National Laboratory, where he had done his research and made friends with the scientists. Their praise of and interest in his work was wonderful, but in a way not that much better than the remark made by Stewart, the son of our local deli owner, who made delicious sandwiches, and who hired Steve to make new signs for the store ("Salami $5.95" etc.). When Steve sold his drawing to the Met and was on the way to deliver it to them, he stopped by the store, and in his excitement and pride showed the drawing to

Stewart and his dad. Later Stewart said to me, "Steve's a really good artist, y'know? Those bone drawings he made? Really makes ya stop and think."

One of the more memorable parties we had in that studio was held sometime in the late 1980s. Our friend Paul Niederman, whom we had known since Steve's early days in the *roulotte,* when it was in Bry-sur-Marne, was a Holocaust survivor. We had not known this for the first few years that we knew him. We did not even know he was Jewish, and certainly had not thought about whether he was or not. The only clue to what he had suffered in his teen years he referred to only once, and in a very vague way, when I asked him one day if he had children. He told me he did not, and added, "I had a very difficult childhood." That was, we later learned, a supreme under-statement. In 1987 he was called upon to testify at the trial of Klaus Barbie, the infamous "Butcher of Lyon." Paul, 16 years old in 1944, was one of a few people who had by good fortune left a shelter for Jewish children in Izieu just days before the Gestapo hauled off all of the inhabitants and sent them to Auschwitz. There was only one survivor from that roundup.

It was very difficult for Paul to face that trial and to testify, but once he did it changed his life forever after; he took his responsibil-ity as a witness to the genocide very seriously. He traveled to Germany frequently to speak to groups, usually school groups. He always told the students about what had happened, and he always stressed that what had happened had nothing to do with them, that they were not responsible. But he wanted them to know, because he wanted it to never happen again.

Anyway. Most of that came later. What happened initially, after he had testified in the trial, is that through the experience of testify-ing, he was reunited with childhood friends, fellow survivors of the camps at Rivesaltes and Gurs, where he and his family had been interned in the South of France. And he asked me and Steve, in around 1988, if we would help him host a reunion for his New York-based friends and fellow survivors.

We were of course both honored and pleased to do so, and we decided the best place to do so was in Steve's studio in the Navy Yard. The only problem was that the Navy Yard, with its chain-link fence security and generally industrial atmosphere was, well, a little bit reminiscent—or could be reminiscent—of a concentration camp. How were we going to deal with that?

Steve came up with the perfect solution. "We're just going to make it really special," he said. He hired a friend who was a professional clarinetist to come with his chamber music group and play live music: we bought food, lots of it, from a caterer, and some of Junior's famous cheesecakes. And we had one of the most extraordinary social events we had ever hosted. That group of survivors was amazing. What they had lived through! And they had retained their humanity and even their sense of humor about it. I remember being so touched, moved, impressed at witnessing them laughing, slapping their knees, making fun of their German captors, mocking their accents ("Vee HAF our WAYS!" was one of the punch lines that sent them all into gales of laughter).

Paul remained a dear friend until the end of his life, and when our children came along, he was like another grandfather to them, which was special for all three of them. After the first couple of years of taking our kids along with us to the farewell dinners we would have in Paris for my students, dinners that were excruciatingly boring for the kids to sit through, I started asking Paul if he would mind taking them out to dinner with him at a local brasserie instead. He always did so.

* * *

I continued reading, and writing, as I worked on my master's degree. Shakespeare. Romantic Poetry. Theater of the Absurd. I was getting to read almost everything I had wanted to thus far, and things I hadn't even thought about. Steve was exhibiting here and there, getting good press—a very favorable review in the *New York Times* for his first one-man show—and life was good. Despite our meager income we got to go to a lot of theater and other arts events through my job at Hunter, which had started out as a clerical position and turned into an administrative one, as the administrative assistant for a new program Hunter was launching called "The Junior Year in New York." I was put in charge of creating a series of cultural and arts events to expose the students who had come from all around the US to the vibrant cultural life of the city—and a perk was that Steve and I got to go with them. We saw lots of wonderful things, and we made some very good friends through that program. The students were full of creative energy and enthusiasm for life in the Big Apple; and many of them had impressive careers ahead of them, among them Steve Inskeep, who became a well-known reporter and anchor at NPR, and Louis Edwards, a talented young writer from Louisiana who became an award-winning novelist. While I've kept in touch with only a few of them, all the ones I know of have gone on to do interesting things, to be good parents, good citizens, good people.

One of the most interesting jobs I had at Hunter was a grant-funded administrative assistant position working with Dorothy James, a Welshwoman who was Chair of the German Department. She had created a very ambitious project for developing a proficiency-based method for the teaching of foreign languages, and she won several major grants from the National Endowment for the Humanities to carry out this work. The basic idea was to create a curriculum that was devoted to developing true proficiency in students of foreign languages, starting from "zero" and slowly helping them build their skills, as opposed to just pretending (after the first four semesters of introductory language teaching) to teach literature to students whose linguistic skills were nowhere near advanced enough to understand literature in a foreign language.

Dorothy and her colleagues worked hard and achieved some impressive success toward this goal in the German Department. It was able to work well in a small department where the principal investigator of the grant was also the department chair: Dorothy was thus able to adjust the reward system within the department to some extent, in order to recognize all the hard work being done on the teaching of language skills and revamping the curriculum. Also, all of the professors in the department taught both language and literature courses, so that "language teachers" were not set apart and disadvantaged, as they usually are, on the promotion and tenure ladder. And everyone in that department, from adjunct lecturers to full professors learned how to apply the principles of proficiency-based teaching.

I enjoyed that work a lot: it was intellectually interesting, and exciting to see the kinds of progress that the professors were making. And it was fun to often serve as the "guinea pig" when professors from the Romance Languages Department would test me in my knowledge and level of oral proficiency in French and in Spanish, as they tried to learn how to use the proficiency scale—which had been initially developed by the Department of Defense—to assess student skill levels in reading, writing, listening, and speaking. This was an important part of the whole project, and it was amusing to see how excited the professors would become when they realized I had just demonstrated "linguistic breakdown" in one of those two languages; that is, when my level of proficiency was simply inadequate to answer a question I had been asked, especially when I provided them with a "classic" example of linguistic failure.

One of my duties in that job was to take minutes at the regular meetings of the faculty who were involved in the project. Once I wrote out the minutes to a meeting that included a verbatim account of a ridiculously circular conversation that had taken place in the meeting, along with my wry comments about the conversation, and some additional ironic commentary. I shared that version of the minutes with Dorothy, who found it very amusing. Then I edited it to create a much less frank, and of course also less amusing, version that could be submitted for the record.

Dorothy and her husband, Tom Settle, who was a professor of the history of science, became good friends of ours, and through the years she has remained for me not only a very good friend, but also a trusted and helpful mentor.

I did typing jobs "on the side" too. Hunter was a good place to find interesting side jobs as a typist. Usually I was typing manuscripts, either for books or dissertations. One was a thesis about the painter Mark Rothko. Another project offered me a peek inside the life of the super-rich in New York, for a client who was married to a wealthy real-estate developer. My client was nice, but I found the peek inside that world unsettling. She and her family lived in a penthouse apartment on Fifth Avenue. I would go to meet with her in their home, usually in the late afternoon, and a maid would come into the room at a certain time of day, simply to draw the curtains as the sun moved low in the sky. I couldn't help wondering, what, my client couldn't have pulled the curtains herself, when the angle of the sun called for it? I was invited to stay to dinner there once, and the meal was served by a maid, which meant that you sat quietly as she spooned food onto your plate from your left side. That was strange and unfamiliar enough, but the thing I will never forget is how at the dinner table that night the discussion found its way to the presence of homeless people in the streets of Manhattan. "Those people don't need to be begging, they have places to be, they have plenty of food," my client's husband told their two children, who were about seven and nine. It was a cold and unfeeling remark, and it was also dishonest; I knew it, and he knew it, and my client knew it, but of course the kids didn't know it. I wasn't about to challenge this man, whom I had only just met, in front of his children while sitting at his table as a guest; but I felt pretty dishonest myself, not saying anything to counter the lie that I could feel hanging heavily in the room. I didn't feel good about my silence.

One of my clients was a woman named Carolyn Eisele. She was a scholar of the history of mathematics, a Hunter alumnus, and a retired Hunter professor. She was also the foremost expert in the world on the American philosopher Charles S. Peirce. She was working on editing the works of Peirce for Harvard University Press, and that is what I was typing for her. She lived in an apartment in a high-rise apartment building near Hunter. I worked with her for quite a while, a couple of years, I think, and we would have good conversations. Mostly she talked and I listened. I knew that she loved music, but I did not know until I was writing this book that as a young woman she had studied voice in Paris, and that apparently her husband was a voice teacher she had met in Los Angeles. She was a kind woman full of deep insight, and obviously extremely intelligent. She was in her late seventies when I worked for her, and was full of life and upbeat energy: she lived until she was ninety-eight. I learned important things from her. I remember her telling me, for example, that a marriage goes through long periods of ups and downs. She had been married for thirty years. "The first ten years were wonderful," she said. "Then there were ten years that were just okay, we were busy doing our work. The last ten years were dreadful, just dreadful. But that's what happens. It's not all good." I don't remember the details of why they were so dreadful, but I think the dreadfulness had to do with her husband's ill health in the end of his life. I understood that she saw in me someone worth trying to teach something about what she had learned about life, and I was honored.

* * *

It was a good life. Steve and I had good and interesting friends, and we had lots of fun with them doing the goofy kinds of things young couples in their twenties do before they have kids. (Many years later I told my kids, who were enjoying watching *Seinfeld* reruns, that it all felt very familiar to me).

When we had been in New York for a few years, I won $400 in an essay writing contest at Hunter and I used the money to have my piano shipped from my friend Cherie's house in Minnesota to us in Brooklyn. "Now we can have a Christmas party," I said. I had over the previous few years been trying to liven up our block at Christmastime; it didn't seem Christmas-y enough to me. I started by stringing lights in our windows, and then Steve started spraying drawings of us and our dogs, and Christmas greetings in the windows with fake snow.

But having a party would be even better. My original idea was to invite friends over for Christmas caroling: we would start with hot cider and sing a few songs at the piano, then go out into the streets to bring "the Christmas spirit" to our neighbors. But we never got around to the caroling. The party grew to include more people, more food, but always there was also singing. I didn't care who could sing well and who was completely tone deaf (and we had some of each): to me it was the singing one's heart out that counted, and we did a lot of that. Our parties came to be an annual event that everyone looked forward to. And even though the money was always tight for us, we always did it. I remember one year I was worried because I didn't feel like we should spend the money for a ham, like we usually did. That year one of our neighbors on the block came bearing a ham: how did he know?

One year we were invited to a Christmas party being held by friends of Steve who were living in Manhattan. One of the friends was a very talented singer/songwriter who had come to New York along with an agent, but she didn't stay long. She probably wasn't really cut out for life in New York. I remember one day she said of me, admiringly, "Janet lives life to the fullest, she takes the subway!"

Anyway, at that one Christmas party, somehow it was mentioned that I could play the piano, and I was invited to sit down to play some Christmas songs for them and their friends, many of whom were actors and actresses working on Broadway. It was an incredible experience, to have that kind of voice power surrounding me while I played my favorite Christmas carols, and theirs too. As a young teenager I had sometimes had the fantasy while playing the piano that somehow (a big somehow!) a talent agent would be walking down Foley Blvd. in Coon Rapids (a road *no one* ever walked on, ever, much less talent agents), and they would hear me playing, and they would think, "Wow, who is *that?!*" and that would be my big break. (But big break for *what*? I never really pursued the rest of that fantasy.) Now here I was, fifteen years later, in New York City, and Broadway had come to me; and those rich, full, fantastic voices were surrounding me at the piano. What a thrill!

* * *

The location we had lucked into, that beautiful block overlooking Ft. Greene Park, was a mixed blessing. The park was beautiful and so were the brownstones, but there was a lot of street crime in the neighborhood: many were the times we threw open the windows when we heard screams in the street. It was a classic haves-and-have-nots situation, the people living in the brownstones having more than the ones who lived in the public housing projects just down the street. And it was a convenient block for muggers, with the park right there providing a ready means of escape. We would shout warnings to the muggers, and call the police. ("Someone's being mugged again.") Once I barely escaped being mugged myself as I moved from the cab I had taken from the subway to our front door, only because Steve looked out the window in time to scare the muggers away.

As my biological clock was ticking, there came a time when we had to decide whether we were going to stay together, marry, start a family, or go our separate ways. As for most struggling artists, for Steve the decision wasn't easy. But on Christmas Eve of 1984 he passed me a note as I left the pew to go forward and receive communion at the 11:00 service: *Will you marry me?* it said, and of course my answer was yes. We were married the following May, in the garden of the Caroline Ladd Pratt House in Brooklyn, a few blocks away from our home. Most of our immediate family came, almost all of our New York friends, and a few special friends from home and college also made it there. It was a beautiful sunny day, with the horse chestnuts at the peak of their blooming, branches swaying gently in the breeze. It felt like the most wonderful day of our lives thus far.

Would that it could have continued "until death did us part," but it didn't turn out that way. However, the children I had longed for came—two of them, two wonderful sons—and they filled both of our lives with incomparable joy. And that fact alone has kept us friends and life partners of a sort long after we stopped living together.

Our family in Minnesota, 2000

Stumbling Toward Fulfillment

One of the good things about being American—as compared, say, to being French—is that you can take basically forever to figure out what you're going to do with your life. One of the downsides is that sometimes it *takes* forever to do so, especially if you don't have a calling—or familial pressure—to take a clear path, such as one leading to a career in the law or medicine.

In my case it didn't take forever, but it did take quite a long time. But slowly, ever so slowly, I made my way—or more precisely, stumbled my way—into my life as a professional writer. Some of the opportunities that came my way were pure serendipity, instances of such unbelievable good fortune that at times it felt more like destiny—though I suppose my stubborn refusal, or simply my inability, to "become" anyone other than who I really was, and my talent for writing (and my lack of talent for very much else) helped.

For example there was the job as editorial, and personal, assistant to Caroline Kennedy. One day in the early fall of 1989 I got a call from my friend Michael, an architect who was working for Edwin Schlossberg Inc., a museum exhibit design company. "Would you like to work for Caroline Kennedy?" Michael asked me. "I don't know, it depends," I said. "Doing what?"

It turned out that Caroline, at the time a recent graduate of Columbia Law School, was planning to write a book with one of her fellow alums, Ellen Alderman, about the Bill of Rights. They had had the idea after taking one of their constitutional law classes. Both Caroline and Ellen had been struck by the stories of everyday people whose lives had been impacted by some aspect of each of the first ten amendments to the Constitution, and the lawsuits that had resulted in those principles being tested in the courts. They wanted to pick one story to bring each of these principles alive, and write a book aimed at general readers.

It was a great idea, which turned into a very fine book, and I was lucky enough to be "there" when Caroline was looking for an editorial assistant to help them with the project. Rather than place a classified ad in the *New York Times,* which would have no doubt brought a deluge of hopeful candidates, she had asked her husband to ask his employees to reach out to their friends and acquaintances and recommend anyone they thought might be good—and trustworthy. And Michael had thought of me.

I said, yes, sure I'd be interested in knowing more. And I put together some kind of resume, and sent it to Michael. Not long afterward, I was called for an interview with Caroline, in her home on Park Avenue.

This is one of those points in life where—not to be overly dramatic, but I don't know what else to say—I simply can't help but wonder if something like destiny has played a role. How strange that I would find myself working for Caroline Kennedy!

Why strange? Well, strange only because, as a child I had been known in my family as "the Kennedy nut."

Like many American children, I had been both fascinated by and enamored of that wonderfully energetic, youthful, idealistic clan: charmed by JFK's handsomeness, the elegance and grace of Jackie Kennedy, Caroline's cute haircut, the pony she rode on the White House lawn, and the French-looking clothes, and especially shoes, she and "John-John" wore. What was not to like, especially for a child being brought up by Democrats?

Like so many Americans young and old I had been shocked and horrified by the assassination of JFK, though perhaps it was not so common for a ten-year-old to have reacted by literally becoming ill, taking to her bed and spending those horrible three days afterward glued to the television. Sometime shortly afterward I had written a rather maudlin letter to Jackie Kennedy, and it had apparently been thought poignant by someone on the White House staff, for they had plucked it out of the piles of letters, and an excerpt from it had been quoted in a Scripps-Howard article that was published, among other places, in the *Cincinnati Enquirer*, on January 15, 1964. ("... Young Americans like Janet Hulstrand of Cincinnati. 'I only have a little flag,' she wrote. 'It costed a quarter but I have it hanging up with black streamers...I think that he was a very nice President, best I ever knew. I know it sounds silly, because when I was born Eisenhower was President. But it's true...'")

My mother first learned about my impending fifteen minutes of fame when a local reporter called her, asking if she were the mother of Janet Hulstrand, where I lived, and so on. "Thank you," the reporter said after she had the information she was looking for, and she was about to hang up, when my mom said, "Wait, what is this for?" "There's going to be an article about the letters written to Jackie Kennedy, and your daughter's letter is quoted in it," the reporter said.

Wow.

I was a minor celebrity in my school for a little while after that. The next day the principal congratulated me on the school intercom, and my next-door neighbor David pointed me out to his second-grade class as we filed by them on our way to lunch. I was proud—I *guess* that was the emotion?—but I was also pretty shy, so it left me with a confusing mixture of feelings.

Anyway, there I was, twenty-five years later, entering the marble lobby of an apartment building on Park Avenue and telling the doorman I had an appointment with Caroline Kennedy. Weird.

Naturally I did not introduce myself to Caroline as a former "Kennedy nut." A natural sense of discretion, plus just plain common sense made me realize that that would hardly be the thing to make her feel comfortable or safe with me. Much later, when I had been working with her for a couple of years and we had an easy camaraderie, I did show her a picture of the Kool-Aid stand I had once set up in our back yard, to raise funds for the Kennedy Library.

The stand included a bulletin board display propped against the picnic table with photos of the Kennedy family, including one of three-year-old Caroline from the cover of *Look* magazine, and a cheap American flag, the kind I had referred to in my letter to Jackie Kennedy, the one I had adorned with construction paper black streamers after the assassination. Caroline looked at the photo, smiled, and quipped, "Did we ever get the money?"

Raising money for the Kennedy Library, 1964

That first day that I met her, I don't know what her initial impression of me was, but I know what mine was of her. As I entered her office at the back of the apartment, my first sight was of her scrambling onto a desk to help a workman who had just dropped a heavy—very heavy—window onto his hand. Caroline jumped into action, raising the window so he could get his hand free. She made sure he was okay, then turned to me and said, "Hi, I'm Caroline, you must be Janet."

Thus ended any absurd fantasies I may have been harboring about the lives of the rich and famous. Caroline may have been rich and famous, but she was above all a kind, decent, generous human being who was not above doing whatever mundane task was set before her. For example, scrambling onto a desk to help a workman in distress. She was, as far as I could see, as the years went by, completely unaffected by "who she was" in the eyes of the world. She was just herself, a good person trying to do her best to make the world a better place. What a good job her mother had done, raising her and her brother in circumstances that could not have been more difficult in terms of achieving such a result.

She must have had a fairly good impression of me also, even though I didn't really have any editorial credentials at that time. The main job was to work with her and Ellen on the book but she also made it clear that she would like to have help with a variety of other tasks and errands, and wanted to make sure that would be okay with me. And of course it was. One of the tasks I did for her after I'd been working with her for about a year was to hand-carry the preschool applications to a handful of nursery schools on the Upper East Side for Caroline and Ed's daughter Rose. These were the extremely selective schools that *le tout* New York was vying for, and the procedure was that if the applicants wanted to have any prayer of admission, the applications had to be hand delivered on, I believe it was September 1, a time when most of the people who were going to be sending their children to these schools—including Caroline—were still spending their time in the Hamptons. So I carried the applications around for Caroline, well really for Rose. "Did you get her into Harvard yet?" she asked when we spoke on the phone later that day.

During the time I worked for her, she and Ellen completed their first book, *In Our Defense: The Bill of Rights in Action*, and began work on a second one. They had thought about doing a book either on the 14th Amendment, or on the evolving area of privacy law. For a while I helped them by clipping articles from the paper that had to do with these issues. The day Caroline told me they had decided to do the privacy book, she grinned and said, "Ed said, 'You're going to be sorry.'" She added, with a wry grin, "I mean, it is a topic about which I personally know nothing whatsoever."

Because of her fame, many people unfairly, and also irrationally (considering the well-known intelligence of her family), assumed that Caroline was not doing her own writing. But she was, and although I was given fulsome credit in the acknowledgements to the book, I always told people that my most important editorial contribution to that book was knowing when to stay out of the way of two good writers who were already doing a good job of editing each other. They were writing their first draft longhand on yellow legal pads, and from that I typed the first draft of the manuscript. I didn't say anything about the work until I was specifically asked by Caroline for my opinion. "You're the first one to read this," she said one day. "What do you think?" Then I told her, truthfully, that I thought it was really good. One day not long after that, I noticed that the word "fungible" had disappeared from one of the chapters, and I left a sticky note on the new version of the manuscript I had left for her to read. "I'm glad you got rid of 'fungible'" I said. "I am SO glad you said that!" Caroline said, with a satisfied smile, adding, "We have been arguing about that word for a while. Ellen kept saying it's a word that any intelligent reader would know, and I did not agree." "You were right," I said. "I am an intelligent reader, and I kept thinking it was some kind of mushroom."

"Jackie O" was still alive when I was working for Caroline (her grandchildren called her "GrandJackie"), and so inevitably the day came when I was in the same room with her. I was at a couple of birthday parties that she was at, the first one for Rose's second birthday, and the last one for Jack Schlossberg's first birthday party, to which I wasn't really invited, but my son Phineas, six months old at the time, was. Caroline and their Irish nanny Elaine had been planning Jack's first birthday celebration with the "help" of his two sisters, Rose, who was five, and Tatiana, who was four. At a certain point Caroline had said, "This is a really nice list, but it seems like there are a lot of four and five-year-old girls invited. Who should we invite for Jack?" There was a momentary silence, both girls thinking hard. Then Rose said, with a bright look, "Well, what about *Phineas*?" I was not working for Caroline anymore, but the girls had no doubt heard about the exciting arrival of Phineas, or perhaps had participated in the preparation of baby gifts for him. And so Phineas was invited to the party, and of course I had to take him. This was in January of 1994, and "GrandJackie" died of cancer in May of that year. So she was already not well. But she was there, sitting quietly to the side as any doting grandmother might do, enjoying the scene, and politely staying out of the way.

The few close-up glimpses I had of Jackie all confirmed my admiration of her as a mother. First of all, she had managed to raise both of her children to be unassuming and unpretentious individuals despite their being in the limelight. She had protected them from danger and raised people who were exceptionally considerate of others and did not have exalted opinions of themselves. One of Caroline's most notable qualities is her talent for witty self-deprecation. Once, when she had received an invitation to speak at an event at the UN she handed me the letter, which gave the details of where she "and her staff" should report on the day in question. She handed it to me with a grin, and said, "Clearly they think I travel with an entourage," and added, "You want to come and block tackle for me?" On one of the first days I worked with her we took the subway to go downtown to the Manhattan office of the Southern Poverty Law Center to borrow some books she needed for her research. We went back on the subway too, each of us carrying a large stack of law books. I noticed that when we were in the subway, a few people seemed to do what looked like double-takes, the language on their faces clear ("Could it be? But no, she wouldn't be in the subway...") Another time we were having lunch in a little café near the law library at Columbia with a friend of hers, and the waitress said to her, "Has anyone ever told you you look like a Kennedy?" "Mmm-hmm," she said, and that was all, until the waitress left. Then she looked at us with a slight shake of her head, and a grin.

One of the things I did for her in the early part of the book project was to call people and ask for various types of information or access to documentation she needed. I mentioned to her one day that sometimes people seemed to make the connection with her name and sometimes they didn't. "And when they do, sometimes it's a good thing, and sometimes it's not," she said matter of factly. None of it meant anything to her. She was just focused on doing the work.

She was also a devoted and engaged mother. One time she and Ed had gone for the weekend to their place on Long Island with Rose and Tatiana, without anyone else to help them, which is somewhat unusual among people who have nannies. I happened to be at the apartment working when they returned. She came in the door, dropped the canvas bag she was holding and said, with a grin, "I never want to see these children again." And though I knew of course she was kidding, there was also a tiny part of me that was a bit aghast that she could say such a thing. (It was the part of me that hadn't had any children yet.)

Of course people wanted to know what her home looked like. I felt that basically it wasn't any of their business, but I thought it was probably okay to tell them that it was the way a home would be decorated if *I* had a big, spacious apartment on Park Avenue. The furniture was comfortable, but not fancy. The rooms were filled with light. And there were a lot of books. While I was working for Caroline she did work with an interior designer to decorate the place. I wasn't told so, but guessed that maybe her mother had pushed the issue ("Caroline, really, you have to do something...") and so she went along with it, but her heart was not in it. One day while we were working together on the book, she got a call letting her know that the designer had arrived for a meeting. She looked at me the way a prisoner looks at a family member when being led back into the clink after a visit. And, like a family member in such a situation, I sat by, helpless, but sympathetic as she was led away. The only thing I remember about the ultimate result of the decorating project is that at the end of it the chairs and sofas were sturdier and more comfortable: and that there was wallpaper in the dining room that had a bookshelf motif. It still was very comfortable, just more expensively furnished, more upholstered, and with better curtains.

Sometime during this period Caroline once offered me a chair that had come from her mother's home that she didn't want. "I'd like to have it, but I'll have to ask Steve," I said. He was always accusing me of cluttering up the place, and it wasn't going to be easy to get that chair from her apartment on Park Avenue to our place in Ft. Greene. So I asked him. "Caroline has a chair of her mother's that she doesn't want, do you want to help me pick it up?" I said. "NO WAY!" was his unequivocal answer. "It's probably one of those uncomfortable, frou-frou chairs like my mom always has, no way, I don't want it." So I (much more politely) relayed the message to Caroline and it went on to someone else. A few years later, when Jackie O's belongings were being auctioned off at Sotheby's I came home from somewhere one night to find a very glum Steve lying on the couch, watching the news on television, and the reports of the ridiculous sums of money being paid for even very small, insignificant items from the estate. "I can't believe it," he said. "We could be millionaires." "Not really," I comforted him. "I would have never tried to cash in on a gift from Caroline like that. And even if I had, it probably wouldn't have worked. It's hers and John's auction, not ours."

It was quite a contrast, going from our Ft. Greene neighborhood, which was only one short block away from some tough housing projects on Myrtle Avenue, to Caroline's home with the marble lobby and the friendly doormen. "Don't you get jealous?" my friend Sam asked me one day. "Not really," I said. "Why would I wish I could be her when I could just as easily be one of those poor women living in the projects on Myrtle Avenue?" This is that lesson I had learned from my mother early in life. When I would express envy at all the games, toys, or whatever other children had, my mother would say. "Janet, all your life there are going to be some people who have more than you, and some people who have less. You might as well be happy with what you have." Wise words indeed, and I never forgot them.

I was working both for Caroline and at Hunter College during the period of my mom's final illness and death. Both of my bosses were most understanding and generous in letting me go to Minnesota to be with her as much as I could manage during that time. The last time I went, when it was clear this was to be the end, I think I was gone for about ten days, because I stayed on to help my dad and my siblings through the immediate aftermath of her death, and to arrange the memorial service, and the burial of her ashes.

Then, when I was finally back in New York, almost immediately I was called for jury duty, and (even worse, for my employers) I was selected for a jury.

I had heard from many friends that the best way *not* to be assigned to a jury was to answer the question about whether you had any family members who were lawyers affirmatively. An affirmative answer to that question, my friends told me, was almost sure to result in your dismissal. So, when the question came, I answered, truthfully, "Yes, an uncle and two cousins." And I added, "I'm also working on a book on the Bill of Rights that is being written by two lawyers."

The lawyer conducting the *voir dire* hesitated for a moment, looked me in the eye, and asked, "Do you think that will interfere with your ability to be a fair and impartial juror?" and so of course I answered truthfully, again. "No."

And I was put on the jury. When I told Caroline about this apologetically ("I thought if I told them I was working on a book being written by two lawyers it might help…") she grinned and said, "Oh, Janet. If I were selecting a jury I would want you to be on it."

And so. At a bad time for my employers (both Caroline and Hunter) I spent several more weeks away from my work, waiting for our jury to be called. This meant, most of the time, sitting in a large room (fortunately there were windows), waiting. It was before the internet, so it wasn't really possible to do any work from there. But it *was* possible to write thank you notes to all the people who had sent us sympathy cards and memorial checks for my mother; and to begin to crawl out of the depth of the experience of losing her, and the resulting numbness and sense of disorientation. So for me it was a blessing.

All during this time, Caroline could have reasonably reduced my pay, but she did not. She was most generous, supportive, and understanding.

The jury I was seated on did eventually get called into court; and we listened to about two and a half days of testimony before the case was settled out of court. It was a civil suit against the City of New York, and I must confess that when I first heard that it was someone suing the city, my knee-jerk thought was that the city was an easy target. However, fair and impartial jurors listen to the testimony, and are charged with overcoming any such prejudicial thoughts.

And so I kept my mind open and listened. The case was brought by a boy in his late teens who had been injured a few years earlier in a fall. He had been playing inside an abandoned building owned by the city and had fallen quite a distance from an open beam. Despite my initial thought, it soon became clear that the city had indeed been negligent; the building had not been kept securely sealed, and that is why this poor boy had been able to get in there, and had fallen, and suffered some brain damage.

The city attorneys must have also realized that the case was not going well, and so they settled. We were called together by the lawyers from both sides, thanked for having performed our civic duty as jurors, and informed that we were now to be dismissed, as the case had been settled out of court. When asked if we had any questions, one of the other jurors, Edith, a woman in her sixties, or maybe seventies, who apparently served on juries not infrequently, said, "Yes, please, can you tell us, *was* the city guilty?" (As if the lawyers had in their possession an envelope in which the answer to the riddle was concealed.) Suppressing any sign of amusement or impatience, the lawyer replied, carefully and kindly. "Well, that is what *you* were going to decide," he said. "But now you don't have to, because the case has been settled out of court."

It was quite interesting, being a member of that little cross section of Brooklyn society, that "jury of one's peers." I really only remember clearly two of the jurors. Edith was one of them. The other one was a very nice, youngish man (in his thirties maybe?) who was voted foreman. I don't know what he did for work: probably some kind of blue-collar job. He took his responsibility as foreman most seriously; each morning when we arrived at the courthouse— we were allowed to go home at night with strict instructions not to discuss the case with anyone—he would report to the clerk at the window and say "The Diaz's are here..." (Diaz being the last name of the plaintiff.)

It was Edith who provided one of the more interesting moments for me during the many hours we spent together sequestered in our jury room, reading newspapers and magazines, idly chatting. One day there was some news about John Kennedy Jr. in one of the tabloids. I don't remember exactly what it was, but it must have had something to do with his passing the New York State bar exam on his third try. Edith's remark was, "John's very handsome, but he's not as smart as Caroline." Of course I held my tongue and maintained a poker face, studiously avoiding the appearance of any interest in the conversation. And of course not telling my fellow jurors that in my opinion it was probably not a lack of intelligence, but a lack of interest in a legal career that had made it so difficult for John to pass the bar.

One of the reasons I had accepted the job with Caroline— besides the inherent interest of working on a book about the Bill of Rights—was that I, and many other people, thought it might "lead to something." I never knew what that "something" might be and I didn't think a lot about it, honestly. I just enjoyed working with her, and of course it brought in income we needed. She was an easygoing and generous boss, and the work was interesting and fun. But when she needed a full-time assistant, though she did offer me the position, I knew I was not the best person for that role—office management was what she really needed, and that is not one of my strengths. Also, I had some medical issues that made changing my insurance a bad idea in those pre-Obamacare days when "pre-existing conditions" kept many people trapped in their jobs. My health insurance was being provided by Hunter College, where I had my other job. So I continued to transcribe the interviews Caroline and Ellen had done for their next book for a while, working from home, and she hired someone who definitely had better management skills than I did for the full-time position.

Marta Sgubin, who had been with the family since Caroline and John were adolescents, and was almost like another mother to them, liked me, and around this time she suggested that maybe I could work part-time for John. Caroline told me about this, and asked me if I would be interested. "I mean, I guess it would be okay if what you want to do is spent all your time organizing someone else's life," she said, which I took not so much as a disparaging remark about the job, but as an encouraging remark about what she thought I should really be doing. I did discuss the possibility of working with John with him on the phone, but we both decided I wasn't really the right person for the job.

The job with Caroline did indeed "lead to something." Unpredictably, indirectly, and through unexpected twists and turns, it led to my first substantive editing assignment, for the brother of one of my coworkers at Hunter. The literary agent he had approached with a manuscript had told him that he needed an editor, and through his sister, who knew that I was doing editorial work for Caroline Kennedy, the brother found me. When the agent saw the work I had done on the manuscript, he offered me the opportunity to work on a memoir Andrew Young was writing, *A Way Out of No Way*. I completed my work on that manuscript and left it in a FedEx envelope on my desk, labeled and ready to go, the night before I went into labor with my first son, and later got a lovely signed copy of the book, along with a note that said, "Dear Janet, You're beautiful, giving birth to Phineas and this book at the same time. Andrew Young."

In the years that followed, the same agent, Lawrence Jordan, gave me lots of additional work, including on Andrew Young's next book, *An Easy Burden*, about his involvement in the Civil Rights movement, and a book by Paul Robeson, Jr., a biography of his father. During several years of work with Paul Robeson Jr., I often thought of my mother. Once, when I was about nineteen, for some reason Paul Robeson's name had come up in conversation when we were at my cousins' house. "Who is that?" I had said. "PAUL ROBESON?!" my mother had said, in a tone of astonishment. "Really?! You really don't know who PAUL ROBESON is?" she had repeated. "No, and I don't know who [some random name I just thought up] is either," I replied, mockingly, then said, "Who is he?" "I can't believe it," she said, shaking her head before she answered my question. "I can't believe you've never heard of Paul Robeson."

Years later, was she able to see, from that window in heaven I have so often wished for in the years since? Could she see her daughter working with Paul Robeson, Jr.? Could she see him coming over to our place in Brooklyn to hand off parts of the manuscript, and discuss things that were bothering him? Could she see him ask the young grandsons she never got to meet, when he arrived one evening to find them bouncing on the sofa and watching a movie about the Titanic, with a barely suppressed grin, "Did it sink yet?"

I hope, oh how I hope that maybe, somehow, she could.

Paul Robeson Jr., me, Lawrence Jordan

The Second Part of Paris

CUNY students in Paris 1998

S teve and I had gone back to France in the winter of 1984 to visit friends. That time, in addition to time spent in Paris and Bry-sur-Marne, we stayed for a few days with Jacques and Josette in their home in Bar-sur-Seine, near Essoyes. We visited *la roulotte*, safely installed in Jacques's storage yard in Essoyes. We had a lovely time with Jacques and Josette, and their two little girls. Then we went on to Italy before returning to the States, telling Jacques and Josette we would be back in six months, believing it ourselves. It made no sense to spend money traveling around the US, especially around New York, we had decided. Better to just save our money and come back over here as soon as we could. Things were cheaper, the food was better, the architecture and history were more interesting, and (at least for me) above all, *they spoke French*!

But what with one thing and another, it would be thirteen years before we made it back again. Steve became very involved in making his sculptures. There were aging and ill parents living in the Midwest to consider when it came to making travel plans: there was not enough money to do everything we wanted to do.

But finally the opportunity came to return to France. I was asked to create a class for the nascent study abroad program at Hunter College. "Think of a place you'd like to go, think of a subject you'd like to teach," my friend Gary Braglia, the visionary engine behind this endeavor said to me more than once, words so magical they didn't seem real, and felt whispered rather than spoken. "Then write me a proposal..."

Gary wasn't even really a friend at the time, he was just the guy across the hall from my office, a graduate student in Russian working out of a storage room the size of a closet. He was trying to open opportunities for CUNY students to participate in exchanges being supported by the US government in the wake of the breakup of the Soviet Union. I'm not sure why he made this offer, but he did, and I will be forever grateful to him for having done so.

The words shimmered somewhere in my subconscious: but the first time he said them to me Phineas was about a year old, and I was so consumed with just trying to keep up with the day-to-day I felt like I didn't even have time to tie my shoes, much less create an interesting, viable proposal for a study abroad class. Fortunately, Gary didn't give up on me. He repeated the invitation, every six months or so, until—though I was by now even more overwhelmed with the day-to-day, with a toddler and a new baby to care for—I was also becoming accustomed to functioning in a state of being overwhelmed. Suddenly, the next time the alluring invitation was spoken, something inside me clicked. "*Why* are we not doing this?!" I said, first to myself, and then to Steve.

So he and I both wrote course proposals. Mine was for a literature class, writing in English about Paris, a class I initially called

"Paris Through the Eyes of Travelers." Steve wrote a proposal for a drawing class. As it happened, my course proposal made it through the vetting process—almost certainly because I had been a student in the English Department's master's program at Hunter, so was known to and loved by the faculty. Steve was not as lucky. The chairman of the Art Department was not going to let anyone who had not been hand-picked by him teach anything, which was unfortunate both for Steve, who would have liked to be able to teach, and for Hunter students, who could have benefited from his teaching as well as the opportunity to study drawing in Paris. (It was not a question of competing with an existing course. There was no existing course. It was simply a matter of protecting academic turf, on principle.)

But Gary made it work for us anyway. He put together a package that allowed us to both go to Paris, and to bring our children with us. Steve would be paid as site director. I would teach my class. The school would provide housing. And so it was that we were launched into the second stage of our lives in France.

Phineas was not yet four. Sam was sixteen months old. A few weeks before we were to fly to France, first Phineas, then Sam came down with the chicken pox. I remember counting the days of Sam's contagious period anxiously, relieved that he would be out of it before we had to fly, though when we got on the plane he was still visibly scarred, making everyone give us a wide berth.

I don't remember the trip very well but I do remember our arrival, how as we rode in a cab into Paris, making a circle around the Place de la Concorde, the Eiffel Tower in view, poor little Sammy threw up on my shoulder. It did not even phase me. "It's a good thing I did not remember how beautiful it is, it would have been too sad to remember that during all the years away," I thought as I covered the spot on my shoulder with a washcloth, and tried to soothe him.

It was my first time teaching anything but a small writing tutorial, the first time I would be teaching a class that required the preparation of lectures, or at least guided discussion. There was jet lag to deal with, of course: even more challenging was looking after two little kids, and dealing with it all in a state of constant exhaustion. Somehow I did it, though I knew it was possible to do better, much better. "I know I could do a better job if I weren't so tired" I remember thinking that whole first year.

That first year the program had been saved from cancellation at the last minute by a contingent of "My Turners." "My Turn" was a CUNY program that allowed senior citizens to take any class they wanted for free if there was space available after regular students had enrolled. And so that first year my class consisted of six My Turners and about eight 18-21-year-olds. Their respect for each other was limited. The My Turners took the name of the program very much to heart and felt that it certainly was Their Turn, to talk, among other things. It was all I could do to keep them from completely dominating class discussions, as the younger set sat sullenly in the front row, sighing and rolling their eyes. Eventually they came to appreciate each other, at least a little bit. I knew I had succeeded in bringing about some kind of *entente cordiale* when they trooped into class on the last day and announced that they had had lots of fun drinking champagne together the night before.

I taught in the mornings and prepared for class in the afternoons and evenings, often at the playground on the Champ de Mars, as the kids played and Steve watched them. There was an antique hand-cranked carousel there, and children were given *batons* with which to spear little metal rings hanging from a post. The first year Sammy was too small to ride on the horses, so we would ride around together in a basket suspended from the center of the carousel, with him in my lap. On those long summer days—it didn't get dark until almost 11 pm—we often stayed out until it was nearly dark, then would trek home along the Avenue Motte Picquet, to our apartment on the Blvd. Garibaldi. Or we would take a shortcut on the rue de Laos, with the elevated tracks of the #6 line of the Metro our beacon: past the Square Cambronne, under the train bridge, and up to our apartment over the Thai restaurant.

It was a sweet and wonderful time, and the best gift of all, at least for me, was that both boys came to love Paris—and France—at a very early age.

Living in Our Nation's Capital

Despite *not* finding a cheap loft in the West Village in 1980, we had managed to stay on in New York for twenty-one years, most of the years happy ones. After Phineas was born, in 1993, Steve decided to go back to school at Brooklyn College, to get his teaching degree. He found work in the New York City public school system but he was *not happy* there. It was clear to me that he couldn't stay in that position forever. He hated it too much, and there were too many years ahead. When he would wake me in the middle of the night to ask, "What are we going to do?" my sleepy answer would be, "I don't know. We'll figure something out..." and I would squeeze his hand. "That's a little vague," he would object. And indeed it was.

Six years before we left New York we had moved from Ft. Greene to Ditmas Park, which was a much more tranquil and less racially tense part of Brooklyn, off Coney Island Avenue. My friends Cheryl and Michael had bought a sprawling three-story home there, and they were renting out the first floor. Phineas was a toddler by then, and I was relieved that we moved out of Ft. Greene before he had to learn that you had to get in the door (quickly!) before someone came up behind you and you were dealt a quick blow to the back of the head, if you were so foolish as not to have your keys at the ready before starting up the steps.

Steve and I have never been accused by anyone of being overly sensible, and we were never very good at *planning* our lives. I remember that shortly after we moved into the house in Ditmas Park, I met our neighbor from across the street when we were both outside early one morning, bringing the empty garbage cans back from the street. She had noticed that we had kids not too much younger than hers, so she came over to introduce herself to me. Even though Phineas was only two at the time, she asked me the very reasonable (for New York) question about what our plan was for school for him. "Mmm, I think our plan is to move to Minnesota," I said. We *were* always kind of planning to move to Minnesota. I remember one day Cheryl (who is also from Minnesota) asked me if this was a real plan, or just "a coping mechanism" for living in New York.

I hadn't really thought about in those terms, but I had to laugh and say, "Probably the latter." There were many things about Minnesota to attract us, but it was hard to tear ourselves away from New York too.

But then out of the blue—well, actually, thanks to a tip from a childhood friend of Steve's—he was presented with the opportunity to take a teaching job—a job teaching sculpture!—in Washington DC, at a fancy private boys' school.

The initial call about the job opening came one day when Steve was at work, teaching at PS 255. I answered the phone. It was a friend of Steve's who had a senior position on the faculty at the school. "Is Stevie there?" he asked me. "No, he's not, can I take a message?" Our friend proceeded to go into a long list of skills that the "3-D" art teacher the school was looking for needed to have, and asked me if "Stevie" could do all those things. "Oh yes, definitely," I said. (I knew he could.) Would he be interested in applying for the job? was the next question. "Oh yes, definitely," I answered, again.

We chatted a bit more, then, before hanging up, I said, "What school is it, again?" There was a brief pause before he answered—we had visited him in Washington, and he was probably wondering how anyone could not remember the name of such a prestigious school—then he said the name of it, and added, "Some people say it's the best school in the country."

While I was very happy about this possible job opportunity for Steve, all of the instincts I had been imbued with from my upbring-ing in the Midwest, the daughter of two modest, hard-working people who had grown up on farms during the Depression, and who were the absolute opposite in every way from elitists, rose quickly to the surface. I suppressed the words that leapt to my tongue automatically and unbidden. But the thought was there: "Well, those people are full of shit," I thought.

Still. This turned out to be the "something" we had been waiting for to get us out of the spot we were in. Steve went to Washington, and he got the job. And so we were moving, not to Minnesota, but to "our Nation's capital."

The sculpture studio in that school was a near-replica of the beloved studio in the Brooklyn Navy Yard Steve had had to dismantle and move into storage in my cousin's barn in Wisconsin seven years earlier, when it became clear that we just couldn't afford it anymore. "They must really love the arts here," we thought: the job seemed too good to be true. And, in a way, as we came to realize over time, it was.

But from our viewpoint then, living in a far too small apartment with two kids and two dogs—tied to the tracks as it were, with a freight train bearing down on us, fast—there was nothing to think about. And so, in the fall of 2001 we moved to Washington. Steve was worried about whether we would be able to make friends in Washington. I was not. (Though I was a bit worried about having to be nice to Republicans: we were arriving in the beginning of George W. Bush's term, after all. When I expressed this fear to my uncle, a former DFL county chair, whom I had urged to run for President when I was ten years old, he smiled and said, "You must just convert them.")

Before it was completely settled that we would be moving to Washington Steve and I went there together to see the house the school would be letting us live in for our first five years in DC. We took the train down there, and it did all seem very idyllic. So clean! So nice! In such a charming Northwest DC neighborhood! Still, when we were back in New York, as we waited on the subway plat-form below Penn Station to take the train to Brooklyn and pick up our kids, we looked at each other, a bit wistfully. "Washington is really nice: but I'm gonna miss the edge of living here, though," I said, looking around the grimy, dingy station. It was indeed grimy and dingy, but it was also filled with such a host of interesting char-acters, sights, and sounds. Steve nodded his head in agreement. New York was gritty, but it also had an energy that we had already noticed was lacking in Washington, or at least was very well hidden.

When we picked up our kids half an hour later in Park Slope, the friend who had taken care of them for us while we were away asked us how we liked Washington. "We liked it a lot," I said. Then added, "But we're gonna kind of miss the edge here anyway."

Our friend, who had grown up in Washington, and was now a lawyer in New York, paused for a second before responding. "Oh, there's plenty of 'edge' in Washington," he said, quietly, and added, meaningfully, "Watch your back."

Words that were prophetic, as it turned out.

We had arrived in DC two weeks to the day before the September 11 attacks on New York and Washington. It was an odd and uncom-fortable time to settle into Washington, and also a strangely wrench-ing time to be away from New York. We grappled with a confused, vague sense of survivor guilt, lessened perhaps by the fact that at least we had moved to a place that had been hit "too."

I was one of the first parents to arrive at John Eaton, the public elementary school in Northwest DC where our kids had been enrolled, to pick them up and bring them home after news of the attacks had broken. I had dropped them off there less than an hour before, and strolled home to the house we had moved into just a few blocks away from both the school where Steve was teaching, and John Eaton. It was such a beautiful day, I will always remember that. I had paused at a house a couple of doors down from us to chat with one of our new neighbors, and I remember that she broke off the conversation because her phone rang. So I continued home, and as I was coming in the door, our phone rang too. It was Steve. "Are you watching TV?" he said. "No, why?" I asked, thinking that was an odd question: I don't watch TV very much. "Something terrible has happened in New York," he said, "Turn the TV on." So I did, and then I told him what I saw. "It's the World Trade Center, it's burning," I said. "What does it look like?" he said. "It looks like a cigarette burning down," I said. I watched for a while, in horror, reporting to Steve what I was seeing and hearing. I don't remember if this was before or after the plane hit the Pentagon, I think probably it was before. But then, across the bottom of the screen I saw the (falsely reported, but in the moment, who knew?) words advising that the National Mall was on fire. "I'm going to get the kids," I told him, and hung up.

Another mom was arriving at the school at the same time I was. I didn't know her; I knew hardly anyone in Washington at that point. "We do take them home, right?" I said to her. "Oh, yes," she said. "When this gets out, it's going to be chaos." I found Phineas first, and his third-grade teacher improvised a very impressive charade that may have fooled some of the other children but didn't fool him at all. "Oh look, Phineas!" she said. "Your mom's here, and you're going to get to have some special time with her today, isn't that nice?" Always possessed of a natural sense of discernment and diplomacy, his eyes narrowed slightly, but he didn't say a word until we had found Sammy also, in his kindergarten class, and were outside of the school, walking toward home. "Mom, what's going on?" he said. "Well," I said, searching for the right words. "Our country has been attacked." I paused, and added, "Some planes flew into some buildings in New York, and a lot of people were killed." He took that in for a moment, then said, "Maybe it was an accident." "Well, it might have been an accident if it was just one plane," I said. "But there were two of them. It seems like it was done on purpose." I paused again. "And also something has happened here, I'm not too sure what. So we're just going home, to be safe." He thought that over, then asked "Who did it?" "We don't know," I said. After another pause, he said "Why would they do that?" and added, "What did we do to them?" I thought then, and I think now, that this response showed exceptional insight in an eight-year-old. "I don't know," I said. "It's never right to hurt innocent people, ever," I added, slowly. "But our country has not always done the right thing. And we must have done something that made someone pretty mad." By now we were walking by the National Cathedral. He looked at it, squinted against the bright light and said, "Do you think they'll try to crash into the Cathedral?" "No," I said, firmly. "I don't think they will." But of course, I wasn't so sure.

I deliberately left the TV off that day; just let the kids play and went through the day in a kind of daze. I remember sitting on my bed after I had fed them lunch and gotten them occupied with something, and thinking, "Man, someone really hates us and wants to kill us all. And there are so many ways they can do that. How will we ever feel safe again?" We went to bed that night with the burden of the confusion, all the bad news and uncertainty of the day weighing heavily on us. What would tomorrow bring? Would Washington be attacked again? Would we even wake up?

But the next day dawned, and it too was a bright and beautiful September day. I opened first one eye, then another. Sunlight was streaming in through the window, across our bed, casting the brick wall it was falling on in a rich golden light. "We're alive," I thought. "We're all still here." And that is the moment when I realized more than I ever had before that that is really all any of us ever have. Waking up, safe and sound, healthy and rested, for one more day of life. Each day a blessing to be grateful for.

One of the first friends our son Sammy made at John Eaton was Aidan Pillard, whose parents are a high-powered pair of constitutional lawyers, David Cole and Nina Pillard. David later became the national legal director of the ACLU, and Nina was appointed to the

D.C. Circuit Court of Appeals by Barack Obama in 2013. In 2001, they were both on the faculty of the Georgetown University School of Law, but I didn't know that yet. I just knew they were lawyers, and that they had one of the most respectful and cooperative parenting relationships I had ever seen. They took turns arranging play dates, and I often saw David sitting on the floor at the Cleveland Park Library, reading quietly to Aidan and his younger sister, Sarah, in the afternoons. He was also often the one who was watching the kids after school, at the Macomb Street playground near the school.

One afternoon shortly after the 9/11 attacks I was at that playground watching our kids, and David was watching his. We were both sitting on a kind of wooden platform for parents to sit on that was built around a tree, and reading the newspaper. I was reading an op-ed that was attempting to defend something George W. Bush had done in response to the 9/11 attacks by comparing him to either Lincoln, or Franklin Roosevelt, to be honest I don't remember which, nor specifically what was being defended. I didn't think much of George Bush, and I was skeptical of the argument, but I knew that I didn't *know* enough to support my skepticism. "I wonder if David would know anything about this," I thought. "He's a lawyer, maybe I should ask him..." *But he could be any kind of lawyer*, the thought came to me. Congratulating myself (silently) for having become *so* much more sophisticated now than I used to be, back when I was just a rube from Coon Rapids, Minnesota, *There are so many kinds of lawyers. He could just be a real estate lawyer, or something* I said to myself, and decided to leave him alone and let him keep reading.

A few nights later I was watching a late-night news program on television. The topic of discussion was protecting civil liberties during a national security crisis. And the invited legal expert was David Cole, that nice parent from the playground and (I then learned) a professor of constitutional law at Georgetown.

Through Aidan and Sammy's friendship, we all became good friends. In fact one of my fondest memories from that time in

Washington—in a way—was Election Night of 2004, when David and Nina and their kids, and another family we were both close to, came to our house for dinner, and to watch the election results together. All of us, adults and kids alike, were feeling hopeful that John Kerry would win the election, and it was all very jolly for a while. I remember one of the high points of the evening being David saying, softly, "I think he's gonna win. I think Kerry's gonna win…"

We had the champagne chilling, but of course David's hopeful prediction did not turn out to be true: the evening went downhill fairly quickly after that, and the champagne remained in its bottle.

It continued to be a strange time, that whole first autumn in Washington. For one thing, without saying so, everyone was waiting for the next attack. It was also that same autumn that, shortly after 9/11, envelopes arrived at our local post office with anthrax powder in them, forcing it to close for at least several days, I don't remember how long, so that it could be decontaminated. Shortly after it reopened I received an envelope one day that looked like it had some dried white powder on it. *Hmm,* I thought. *Okay, now what?* I picked up the flyer that had been delivered to our house with instructions for what to do if you received a suspicious letter. The instructions were to call local law enforcement. And so I called our precinct. "I've just received a letter that came through the Friendship post office," I said. "It is not from a suspicious source, it is from my mother-in-law." (It was an orange envelope addressed to one of our sons: no doubt a Halloween card and a $5 bill were inside.) "But it does have what looks like the residue of white powder on the outside of the envelope. What should I do?" I asked.

"Take it to the post office," I was told.

Stunned at this response, I waited a couple of seconds before answering. "Well, I'm not too sure they would want me to come walking in there with a possibly tainted letter after they have just been able to reopen, after having just thoroughly decontaminated the place," I said.

There was now a pause on the other end of the line. "Okay," the person answered. "Where are you? We'll come and get it."

And sure enough, within a quarter of an hour a large industrial truck drove up to our house and a man wearing a heavy-duty oxygen mask and dressed in a moon suit, approached our front door, holding a large plastic bag in front of him with the help of a metal pincher. "Put it in here," he said through the mask, and I dropped it in.

The following year was the autumn of the sniper who terrorized the Washington suburbs with a string of random shootings. Once again it was a gorgeous autumn, with mild, summery days; but the children at John Eaton were kept inside at recess time, for fear that the sniper might begin to attack within the District, though none of the shootings had taken place within the city boundaries. Many parents stopped walking with their kids to school during those weeks, but Sammy and I continued to walk the ten or so blocks from our home to the school every morning and walked back home again every day after school. I remember seeing a news article that described this type of activity as "an act of courage." It didn't seem like an act of courage to me, it seemed like the only sensible thing to do, at least unless and until the attacker changed his geographic M.O. (The sniper was only picking targets outside of the city limits.) One day as I was waiting to pick Sammy up after school, one of his classmates, a sweet little girl confided to me, "We can't play outside because of the sniper." She paused, then added, "We don't know his name. So we're just calling him 'the sniper' for now." Eventually the sniper was apprehended and the kids were able to play outside again.

* * *

"If you want a friend in Washington, you'd better have a dog," Harry Truman said, famously. I didn't remember these words until we'd been there for a while, but eventually I came to understand why he had said them. I also remember thinking, in a kind of *ah-hah* moment after we had been living there for a couple of years, that

Washington must be the place people were talking about when they said, "It's a wonderful place to visit, but I wouldn't want to live there."

Washington is *not* a friendly town. But I didn't know that when we moved there. I moved there with an open mind and an enthusiastic spirit. I had always loved visiting Washington: it is a beautiful city, and so much cleaner than New York; and there are all those wonderful museums. From the perspective of my Midwestern roots, it seemed to me that Washington and New York were probably like two sides of the same coin. A lot of really smart, really ambitious people who had been drawn there for one reason or another, people with dreams and with plans. I remember thinking that it was probably a lot like New York, "except more people involved in government." What I didn't know is how much of a difference that would make in the character of the place. And I hadn't really thought about the fact that actually two sides of the same coin are always distinctively different.

In any case, after a couple of years of living in Washington, I saw what Harry Truman had meant. I should have had more of a clue when the headmaster of the school where Steve was teaching let us know that artists and writers were not exactly sought-after personages in the social world of Washington. We had been summoned to his office the spring before Phineas was to enter fourth grade—the year when most of the elite private schools begin. We had been in Washington for less than a year at this point. Phineas had taken the entrance exams and been invited to join the class of 2011. As a "faculty child" he would be able to attend there tuition-free. We weren't 100 percent sure we wanted him to go there: what would it be like, being a "faculty kid" in a place where many of the parents were senators, wealthy lobbyists, impressive journalists, even some Arab sheiks? Where everyone, or almost everyone, had a swimming pool, fancy cars, and the like? But we also knew that educationally speaking this was a great opportunity for him. We had led Phineas to believe that the decision was his, whether he wanted to go there or not, explaining away the tests he had to take by saying that the teachers needed to know who knew what, since everyone would be coming from different schools.

We were told that the headmaster was meeting with all the faculty parents whose sons had been accepted for the following year—I think there were two or three boys that year. Perhaps the real purpose of the meeting was to dissuade us from taking them up on the offer. In any case, in the middle of the conversation, the headmaster had casually remarked that it might be a bit difficult for us socially. "I mean, as a writer and an artist you're not going to be invited to dinner parties in Potomac," he said.

We looked at each other blankly for a moment, trying to think what "Potomac" was, and wondering why we would care about this. (We later learned that Potomac was a wealthy Maryland suburb of Washington.) "Well," we both said after a moment of thought. "We don't really care about things like that." We were a bit nonplussed, though. A place where talented, interesting people actually had a *negative* social status? It was a weird moment.

If the headmaster's intention had been to get us to save the school thousands of dollars by not enrolling our son there, he would have done better to point out that, with a late July birthday Phineas would be one of the youngest boys in the class. Many DC boys whose birthdays were in the late summer or early fall were "held back" for a year before they started to school in order to avoid such a fate, since in a place where sports were of paramount importance, to be the youngest, thus behind the growing curve, could be a distinct disadvantage during adolescence. But the headmaster didn't mention anything about that. He expressed some concern about Phineas's ability to keep up academically, but we knew there would be no problem there. He had always been ahead of his age that way.

And so, for better or worse, our boy began going to school in the place that had the dining hall that looked like Hogwarts, in the fall of 2002. Steve and I agreed that if it turned out not to be good for him, we would take him out of there. But mostly, it turned out to be for the better.

It was true about our negative social status, however. We basically weren't invited anywhere, even by Steve's friend who had recommended him for the job in the first place. When our first Thanksgiving in DC was approaching and we hadn't been invited to join anyone, we decided to accept one of the several invitations we did have, to celebrate with friends in New York who missed us. Spectacularly, the friend who had invited Steve to apply for his job, and who lived in the other half of the duplex we were living in, had a Christmas party that year, and he didn't invite us to that either. Clearly we had done something wrong, but we never knew what it was. Was it the moving company we had chosen, with the cheeky, New-York-ish company name? (Schlepper something, I think. Super Schleppers?)

We'll never know. All we know is that before we had had a chance, really, to do *anything* wrong, we were already being shunned by Washington society. (It must be admitted that while we were clearly being "dissed" by Washington society, we weren't all that interested in or impressed by Washington society either. So in a way it was perfectly fair.)

But it was also weird. Neither Steve nor I had ever been very comfortable at cocktail parties, but in Washington the discomfort went to a new level. Unlike in New York, in Washington it was not enough to be an interesting person, and to get over your shyness in order to sustain a conversation. In Washington you had the distinct impression that on being introduced to someone—or introducing yourself—you had less than five seconds to let them know whether or not you were worth talking to. The question on everyone's mind, it seemed, was not, "Who is this person, and what is interesting about them?" but "What can this person do for me?" (Later we learned that this was often expressed in the question of whether or not the person was "a player.") If the answer was "Nothing," or "No, not a player," they were on to the next person. But, again, I have to admit that this actually was a two-way street. In trying to explain the social scene in DC to friends back in New York after we'd been in Washington for a year or so, Steve said, "The problem at these parties is that half of the people are doing something that is *not that interesting*. And the other half won't tell you what they do!"

* * *

One of the more interesting editorial projects I had while living in Washington was editing the annual report for a federal agency that was under the umbrella of the Director of National Intelligence. It was a good idea; basically this agency had been formed after 9/11 to attempt to remedy the situation that had occurred on 9/11, of the insufficient coordination and cooperation among federal, state, and local agencies that had caused a devastating lack of "connecting the dots" and thus caught the US so unaware and unprepared.

I found out about their need for a freelance editor through one of the professional organizations I belonged to, and sent my resume and a cover letter to the program manager who was directing the search. The timing was not great: I was going to drive to Minnesota in less than a week, and the email had said candidates must be available for an in-person interview sometime "soon."

I needed the money very badly (as always) and so I just held my breath that I would be able to make it to a meeting if they called me for one. I didn't say anything about the fact that I would be leaving town soon: it wasn't really their business, I decided, and in any case, since the work would be done remotely it shouldn't really matter to them where I would be doing it from.

Luck was with me, and soon enough I was called to a meeting to be held in an office building somewhere in Foggy Bottom, not far from the State Department. I assumed I would be meeting with just one person, the one who I had been corresponding with, but when I got there, there were two surprises. One, I was asked to leave my cellphone in a small lock box before getting into the elevator. And two, when I entered the room, I was faced with a long table full of men in suits, and was told the meeting would begin when "the Ambassador" arrived.

Wow. Just another one of those moments when I realized I wasn't living in Coon Rapids anymore.

I later learned that the Ambassador we were waiting for was a *former* ambassador, so now I knew another little bit of Washington protocol. ("Once an ambassador, always an ambassador, I guess..." I thought.)

Anyway. They were all very nice, and they decided they wanted to hire me for the job. At that point I did tell them that I would be going on the road soon, but that there was no reason I couldn't do the work from where I was going, and along the way, and that I could meet their deadline with no problem. (The "no problem" part of that wasn't quite true: but that was *my* problem, not theirs. I knew I would find a way to get the work done, and I did, sometimes working in the bathroom of a motel room while my children slept.)

A few days into our westward journey, I got a voicemail from my contact at the agency, who left a message asking me to return his call, which I did, from a roadside rest stop. "Where are you now?" he asked, with what seemed to me a bit of bemusement in his voice.

I was **so** tempted to say, "Well surely you know where I am, don't you?" but I suppressed the urge, not wanting to seem insolent, and said simply, "Wisconsin."

I edited the annual report for them for a few years, and it was very nice working for that team. They appreciated my work, and they were very considerate about telling me so. They even treated me to lunch in a nice restaurant a few years into that relationship, as a way of thanking me, and the director of the agency called me into his office to thank me personally. He was supposed to join the lunch that day, but something "came up." I imagine something often comes up when you're in that line of work.

* * *

I ended up living in Washington for nearly fourteen years, but I never in all that time felt that it was home. I never had the feeling of happy return when flying into one of the Washington airports that I always did returning to New York, or to Minneapolis, or to Paris. I never felt home at all until I opened the door of our house and was inside. In fact the most typical feeling I had on reapproaching Washington when I had been somewhere else, was a kind of dread, and a closing in. I remember distinctly that feeling on returning to Washington from a trip to New York, and attending the annual Christmas party for faculty and their families at the school the first year we were there. It was a nice gesture, that the school gave a party for faculty families. But the stiffness of the affair, on returning from the freewheeling, chaotic spirit of *joie de vivre* that I always feel in New York, was a stark contrast, and it was suffocating.

After about ten years, I realized that if I didn't feel at home in Washington by now, I was never going to. The scene at the private school remained strained until the end. We had two boys there, three years apart: it was somewhat better for Phineas socially, because his class had a friendlier, more welcoming set of parents. (As any parent of more than one child knows, each class has its own particular social dynamic, and some are just nicer than others. Phineas was the lucky one in this regard.) In both cases, I tried to engage: I went to the cocktail parties for the parents almost religiously because I knew that was part of being a good parent, to get to know the parents of your children's classmates. I also needed new friends! And in both classes, of course, there were some nice people. So I persisted. I kept trying, until once, I think it was in the fall of Sam's senior year, as I was driving to yet another parent cocktail party, and a feeling of dread began to grip me as I approached the school. I finally said to myself, "Why am I doing this? If this one particular couple, or that one particular mom are not there tonight, no one will bother to talk to me. What's the point?" And I kept driving, to the home of a friend Sammy had made in kindergarten in the public school, whose mother had become my best friend in Washington.

It wasn't as if there were no progress at all. At the last Parent Dinner I attended, when Sammy was a senior, I found myself seated next to some fourth grade parents at a table where those parents who had not been eagerly invited to sit elsewhere seemed to have ended up. To my astonishment, the senator's wife who had never paid any attention to me in the previous eight years of our boys being in school together came and sat down next to me, and enthusiastically greeted me. (Not by name, though. She probably didn't know my name; it wasn't a name that mattered.) When I told Sammy about this the next day, his wry remark was, "She wanted something." "Yes, obviously, but what could she have possibly wanted *from me?!*" I replied. We both surmised that somehow her social status had fallen—for one thing, as Sammy reminded me, she was not a senator's wife anymore—and what she wanted that night, probably, was nothing more than someone to sit next to. Such is the loyalty of Washingtonians.

This is the same woman who, at the *de rigueur* back-to-school class swim party when the boys were in, I think, eighth grade or so (long enough for the moms to know a little bit about each other if they cared to), had come up to me at the party and said, huffily, "Do you know that your nanny *held up the line?* She *held up the line!*" She was referring to the line of cars in which mothers (and nannies, I suppose) waited for the boys to be dismissed from school and transported them from there to the pool party. "Um," I said. "I don't have a nanny..." The senator's wife looked momentarily half puzzled, half annoyed. Then she simply turned her back on me, and went off to talk with someone else. I realized that she had made the mistake of thinking that the car in which my son was riding was being driven by a nanny. In fact it was being driven by the mother of one of the African-American boys in Sam's class; this mother was one of the few people I could count on to have interesting and sympathetic conversations with at these parties.

This is not to say that I didn't make any good friends in Washington, nor that Washington was short on wonderful people. There are plenty of interesting and wonderful people in Washington, and I met a lot of them, and made some dear friends who will be friends for life, some of them even at that school. But the social climate was always difficult, and it was even more difficult after Steve and I had separated, because despite the very high divorce rate, it was all about couples in Washington. Fortunately, once I was over the initial pain of our breakup, being more or less on my own was, most of the time, okay. By this time in my life I knew that it made a lot more sense to stay home happily reading and writing than to wish I had been invited to dinner parties. (Never mind dinner parties in Potomac. Just *any* dinner parties, anywhere.) I learned to cultivate and appreciate the social circles that welcomed me—mostly other single women "of a certain age"—and to be happy with that. And I concentrated on my kids, my work, and enjoyed the company of the friends I had made, most of them through those several years Sammy had spent in public school. (And yes; I enjoyed the company of my dog.) I also had a very nice, and very interesting neighbor across the street in Silver Spring, where I lived for the last eight years I was in the area, who was also a single woman "of a certain age." She often had barbecues on her screened-in porch, barbecues that felt comfortably Midwestern to me (she was from Illinois); I always felt welcome there, and happy. We had interesting conversations about a wide variety of things, and it was always fun meeting her friends.

There was also the work I did as a member of the planning committee for the American Writers Museum. In 2011 there was an AWP conference in Washington and someone asked me if I was going to go. (AWP is the Association of American Writers and Writing Programs.) To be honest, that is the first time I had heard of AWP, but I did decide to go. Another friend told me there was going to be a presentation by a small group of people who wanted to create an American Writers Museum; a friend of hers was on the planning committee. "Go to their presentation," she said. "They're trying to get more people interested." I went to the presentation and was really impressed with the team, which was headed by an Irishman named Malcolm O'Hagan who had spent his adulthood working on the business side of engineering in Washington. The museum was his idea. On one of his visits back home to Ireland he had visited the Dublin Writers Museum, and when he returned to the US he started asking people where the American Writers Museum was. Inevitably the response would be a kind of groping as people tried to remember where it was. Surely it was on the mall in Washington, along with all the other national museums, no?

But as it turned out, there wasn't one. And so, in that wonderfully American way, we finally got one, more than 200 years into our history, and when we did, it was thanks to an Irish immigrant; an engineer who loved literature, especially Irish literature and American literature (Steinbeck was a favorite of his).

The way I came to be on the planning committee is that I asked them why they weren't on Twitter. "Ummmm…" was their reply. None of them really knew what Twitter was. "I could come and explain to you what it is and how it works. And then if you want, I could get an account going for you," I said. "It's a great way to build an audience," I added. So they invited me to come to one of their meetings, and present the idea. Afterward they invited me to be on the planning committee, and they let me start tweeting for them. I helped edit some of their early written documents too. It was a pretty interesting process to be involved with such a group, occasionally having to defend the use (or nonuse) of a comma, or to explain/defend the subtle differences between "which" and "that." I wish I had been involved with them early enough to explain why naming it the American Writers Museum presented some potential for misunderstandings, if it was really a museum of writers from the United States. But whatever. It opened in 2017, and it is a wonderful institution, located in Chicago.

I believe it was during that same conference that the planning committee for the museum hosted a cocktail party in some fancy office building on 16th Street. That was one of the few cocktail parties I attended during the whole time I lived in Washington that made me feel like I was in New York again. There were interesting people to talk to, not necessarily writers, just people who liked to read and had things to talk about other than their jobs; and there was someone there who was interested in talking to me, about books.

During the last few years I was in DC, I had the opportunity to teach classes at Politics and Prose bookstore, and that became the most joyful part of my existence in Washington, other than my life with my children. Susan Coll, a novelist whose work I admire, had just started working there and was building a program of classes at the store. I proposed to teach a version of the class I had been teaching in Paris for Queens College: she quickly and enthusiastically accepted my proposal, and eventually she became a real friend, introducing me to other people who also became friends; and she was a wonderful supporter of my work there.

The first "Paris: A Literary Adventure" class was a great success—because of the great demand for it, two sections were offered, one in the afternoon and one in the evening. I went on to teach a great many classes there, and this became for me a welcome additional source of income and, even more importantly, a satisfactory substitute for the social life I didn't really have in Washington—not to mention the opportunity to meet fellow Francophiles. I met a lot of wonderful people that way. Most of my students were retired, many of them from a variety of interesting careers (though, not surprisingly, a disproportionate number of my students were either retired or practicing attorneys). This presented me with a really challenging, actually an excitingly challenging situation. You never knew who was going to know what about some arcane topic that was tangential to the discussion: Rocket science? Military strategy? Espionage? Foreign service? So it was best always not to pretend that you knew more than you did, nor to try to be an ultimate authority on anything. This fit both my personality and my teaching style perfectly.

A couple of years into this experience, I was a bit startled to see the names of English and Elaine Showalter on my class list. The extent of my academic credentials, after all, was a master's degree in English from Hunter College. So to say that I was outranked by this academically prestigious couple—she a prominent feminist literary scholar and Princeton professor emeritus, he a prominent scholar of 18th-century French literature, and a past president of the Modern Language Association—is something of an understatement. "Hmm," I thought when I saw their names. "This is interesting. *I* am going to teach *them?!*" There was nothing to do about it, however, other than to decide whether or not to be intimidated. I decided the best thing to do was the latter. "I'll just be myself, and hope they like me," I thought. Fortunately, they did like me, and they were wonderful members of the class. And despite their obvious superiority in terms of academic credentials, they seemed to appreciate what I was doing with the class, which included people from a wide range of walks of life, some very sophisticated in their literary tastes, others not at all. And after the class was over, they extended true friendship to me. They invited me to dinner in their home, to a book party they held for a friend, to the opening of a film their son had directed. In short, they *included me* in their world, and were always kind to me. And I must say that their respect for and belief in me went a long way toward making me feel better about the generally low esteem in which I was held in Washington, especially since their world was one I had a lot more respect for than the world from which I was being excluded.

I had been encouraged by several of my professors at Hunter to continue my studies and get a PhD. And though I would have loved to have continued that life of reading and writing within the academic world—most particularly I would have liked to learn a lot more about American history than I have been able to do—I decided not to follow that path, for two reasons. One is that it didn't seem to me to be a particularly auspicious moment for a white woman to pursue an academic career in the humanities. Things were being balanced; a more ethnically diverse faculty was being actively sought, and I believe rightfully so. The other reason is that by the time I had completed my master's degree, I had sat in a great many academic meetings in my role of various support positions, taking notes and minutes, and thus had seen close up how people within that world often treated each other. I didn't think I wanted to make my life—or have my self-esteem—dependent upon that world. All that backbiting and undermining and—as the joke goes—the stakes are so low!

And so although it meant that I never had the stability of an academic position, it did mean that I have had complete freedom to follow my own path and engage in pure pursuit of my own unique literary interests. In any case my doubts about the likelihood of a stable academic career for me proved to be true not only for white women in the humanities, but for academics in general as institutions relied more and more heavily on adjunct faculty, working them harder and harder; and the road to tenure became more and more difficult for everyone. I have been very lucky to be able to create the literary classes I have created both inside academia as an adjunct professor of English, and outside of it, as a teacher in a wonderful independent bookstore. Although it has rankled at times to know that I'm viewed as a "nobody" by many in the literary establishment, including in the publishing world, I've gotten tremendous satisfaction from the hundreds of students who have appreciated my teaching; and I've been able to spend a lot of my time, though not all of it, reading, writing, and learning about the topics that most interest me. I really wouldn't have it any other way.

Waving to David Downie from Politics & Prose bookstore, after a Skype chat

Interludes Outside the Bubble

We didn't want our boys to be limited to the very insular world of the private school they were attending in Washington. I wanted them to know that that wasn't the real world, or at least that it was only a very small part of it. Going to France every summer for at least a month, usually longer, helped. Taking them to New York on a regular basis to see their friends, and just spend time there helped too. But what helped even more, I think, were the annual trips to Minnesota once we had returned from France. The CUNY program in Paris was for the month of July, which meant that when we got back to the US there was usually almost a month before school would begin again.

Our annual trips to the Midwest had started even before we had moved to that insular world of Washington. It struck me one day in early August when we had returned from France. The kids were with their babysitter at the park and I was working from our home in Brooklyn. I suddenly noticed that I heard something unusual, and I went to the door to see what it was. It was silence! Everyone on the block seemed to have taken off for somewhere. "What are *we* doing here?" I said to myself. And I decided that since I could take my work with me anywhere, it would make a great deal of sense for us to go somewhere else during August too.

And so we developed the habit of going to the Midwest every summer. We found a place to rent on Norway Lake in west central Minnesota, a fifteen-minute stroll down the lakefront road to the home of one of my best friends, and a fifteen-minute drive to visit my cousin, who had a beautiful old farmhouse set "in the middle of nowhere," a very nice husband who was a collector of antique cameras and tractors, and a son about the same age as our boys. We would return from Paris, dump our bags, wash our clothes, repack, and then pile into the car and head west, making stops along the way in Michigan and Indiana to see aunts, uncles, and cousins, and then Steve's mom in the suburbs of Chicago before heading on to Minnesota.

Phineas was only in the fourth grade, his first year at the private school in Washington, when he came home one day and said, "Mom, what's Ivy League?" I paused before answering, and then I said, "It's a handful of colleges—just a very few of them—that are very good schools." Paused again. Continued, choosing my words carefully. "Some people think that it is extremely important to go to one of them. But we don't think that." Another pause. "When you're old enough to go to college, if you want to try to go to one of them you can, and we will help you. But they are very very hard to get into. And there are many other *really* good places to go to school. So it doesn't really matter if you go to one of them or not. It just doesn't."

He took all that in, said, "Oh." And then went out to shoot baskets in the alley.

By the time he was old enough to apply to schools he had decided that he didn't really even want to apply to any of the Ivy's. By then I think he had decided for himself that he wanted to be exposed to a little bit wider world and not be surrounded by the same kind of people he'd already spent so much time with at his private school. He chose to apply to about ten of those other "really good" schools and was accepted at nearly all of them. When he showed me the essay he had written for Macalester College in St. Paul, which began by recounting his memories of summers in France, and then led into, "But the best part of the summer was when we went to see my cousins in Minnesota…" I knew *that* would go over well. And indeed that is where he ended up, and he was very happy there.

Sam had asked me about colleges also, at an even younger age. I think he was about five when out of the blue one day he said, "Do you have to move away from home to go to college?" "No," I said.

"Most places have colleges nearby, so you wouldn't have to move away if you didn't want to. So you can stay with us as long as you want to." Then I added, "By the time you're that old you probably will *want* to go away to school, though." He mulled this over a bit and then said, "I think I want to stay with you until I finish college. And then I've **got** to be going."

When we were still living in Brooklyn, thanks to financial aid we had been able to send our kids to Berkeley-Carroll, a wonderful private school in Park Slope. (Yes, we filled out financial aid forms for *preschool!*) I felt a little bit funny about doing that until I got to the question where you had to declare your assets and we were asked if we had a boat. ("You mean there are people asking for financial aid who have *boats?*" I thought.)

Berkeley Carroll was a wonderful school but one thing they didn't have that we really wanted for our kids was foreign language instruction at the preschool level. So, together with a group of parents we advocated for an afterschool French language program of some kind, and the school agreed to set one up. Phineas was four when it began, and he was not one bit interested in learning French. I decided to resort to that often very effective parental technique of bribery. "I think you'll like it," I said. "But if you agree to go, I'll give you a Pokemon card every time after class." As he came marching out of the classroom with his little friends after the first session, he held out his hand, and scowled at me as he closed his fist around the card. "And I *didn't* like it," he hissed. (Always the diplomat, he did say it quietly.)

But he did like it. The school had found a nice young Frenchman to teach the class and he knew how to make things fun for four and five-year-olds who had already been in school all day. A few times after the first class, when Phineas came skipping out of the room, I said, "How was it, was it fun?" "Yes!" he said. "We got to play *sous la table et sur la table.*" The young Frenchman had correctly perceived that these kids needed movement, and so he devised a way to combine intellectual learning with kinesthetic activity, by inviting them to either climb *sur la table* or scoot *sous la table*. They loved it!

And so we found ways to work around the fact that we were living in a very insular world. We just left there for as much of the year as we could.

A Place to Call Our Own

An important thing to know for the purposes of *this* story is that Washington DC is unaffordable for many people, especially for teachers of sculpture who are married to freelance writer/editors. As part of the package offered by the school, we had been given a place to live for the first five years in a house owned by the school, which made DC affordable for us for those first five years, and gave us a head start on the next few.

We had had so much good luck in our lives that we foolishly, naively believed that after five years, either we would have been able to succeed well enough in Washington to afford to buy a house, or the school would love us so much (didn't most everyone love us?) that they would let us stay longer.

But "the school" didn't love us as much as we had thought they would. We weren't the type to be invited to dinner parties in Potomac, after all; and not only that, but Steve was a sometimes undiplomatic, always adamant defender of his art program at a school that was much more heavily invested in sports and academics than art. The spaciousness of the "three-D" art studio and the expensive equipment therein had given us the initial impression that at this school the arts were very important. But what was important, really, was *giving that impression*, not necessarily the reality, as we learned all too well eventually.

So when the five years were up in the spring of 2006 we had to move, and we had to move into a housing market that was at an all-time high. The "housing bubble" that would burst and drive the country into a deep recession, and threaten to bring down the whole economy was still two years away. But the early signs were there to those in the know. I remember sitting on the bleachers in a gymnasium watching one of my sons play basketball one Saturday morning, probably sometime during that same spring. Two other parents from the school Steve was teaching at were sitting near me, watching their boys play. I knew very little about them, but I knew they were both involved somehow in the world of finance. "Did you hear about the subprimes?" one of them murmured to the other. No answer, just a solemn nod as the other person looked straight ahead. "Who's gonna pay?" was the next question, also pronounced in a hushed tone.

I had no idea what the word "subprime" meant, or what he was referring to. But I knew, instinctively, that the answer to the question was "We are."

Still blissfully unaware, however, we tried to enter that market. We had enough money to think about buying a house for the first time in our lives, and so we did. We looked around, and we even bid on a couple of places, not in Washington, which we could definitely not afford, but in Takoma Park, Maryland, a nearby suburb. We were totally naive, and operating in a cutthroat environment. It is perhaps one of the greatest strokes of luck in our fortunate lives that neither of the two bids we offered made the mark and somehow we were smart enough not to respond to the encouragement of our realtor to "go for broke." (Because, buying at that time, at those prices, with those rates, that is exactly what we would have done.)

Fortunately, two different friends, both of whom had far more real-estate smarts than we did, cautioned us. "I think if I were you I would let someone else take the risk right now. I think you should rent," one of them said. "If you absolutely love Washington and you know *for sure* that you want to live here for at least the next thirty years, and you have no doubts about that *at all*, go ahead and buy," the other one said, adding, "You'll probably be able to wait out whatever happens."

As this did not very accurately describe either our feelings about Washington or our thoughts about the future, we decided to rent.

But we had that little nest-egg and we had the desire to own something. It is a fairly natural desire, after all, and also there is something about turning fifty that makes people feel that there are certain things in life they really should have achieved by now. Owning a home is one of them.

And that is how we came to have the house in France. It's a complicated story, and one I will not tell right now—that is for another book. Suffice it to say, we found a lovely home in Essoyes, the lovely little village in Champagne where we had first fallen in love with each other, and with France. And we bought it together.

Then, about a year later, we broke up.

Our dream home in Essoyes

Reclaiming the Roulotte

La roulotte 2007

Back in 1997, a few weeks into our first year of running the study abroad program in Paris, with the students stabilized and on their own on the weekends, we had rented a car and returned to Essoyes. On the way, we stopped to see our friend Jean-Lou at his family home in Loches, the village just before Essoyes, and there, to our surprise, we saw *la roulotte*, now parked in his garden and looking a bit—well, actually, a lot—the worse for wear. "What happened?" Steve said.

What had happened is that sometime during the thirteen years of our absence, the *roulotte* had been broken into and vandalized—very likely by gypsies, though no one knows for sure who did it. Whoever was responsible for the attack, they did it with gusto; they ripped the shutters off and smashed the windows, broke the beautiful wooden front doors, took anything of value—though there wasn't much—and left the *roulotte* in a very sorry state.

Dismayed at what had happened, Jacques asked Jean-Lou if he could keep the *roulotte* at his home in Loches, where it would be safe from further destruction. Jean Lou readily agreed to do so, and they hauled the *roulotte* to his family's home, where he sealed it up against further rain damage. And there she had sat, in her forlorn condition, for several more years, awaiting our return.

But of course we still weren't able to do much about it. We were only in Paris for a few weeks, and anyway where could it go other than where it was? And so it sat in Jean-Lou's family's garden for another ten years.

Then we bought our house, our dream house, in Essoyes, just four kilometers away, and the dream house had a very big yard, with plenty of space for *la roulotte*. The very first weekend after we had signed the papers and the house was really ours, Steve announced that we were going to see Jean-Lou, to see about the possibility of getting the *roulotte* back.

"I'd love to have it again," he said. "But I can't really expect him to give it back. He's had it all this time."

Still, he wanted to ask.

It was a Sunday afternoon, the part of the afternoon after one of those lingering French meals when the dessert had been served and it was on to coffee and more talk. It was a beautiful, sunny day, and as usual there was an assortment of people, some of Jean-Lou's friends, siblings, grandchildren hanging around, his ancient mother seated as always at the head of the table. We were invited to sit down and join them, and so we did. And we talked about this and about that.

Eventually Steve had the courage to pose his question. When there was a pause in the conversation, he took a deep breath and said, "Um, Jean-Lou, there is something I have to ask you, and I want you to be honest with me." He paused again. The room had become still. "I would like—if it's okay with you, and *only* if it's okay with you—now that I have a place I can put the *roulotte,* I'd like to take her back. If it's okay with you. If there's not a problem with that." He stopped talking, winced slightly, then waited for the reply.

There was a long moment of silence, all eyes moving from Jean-Lou, to Steve, back to Jean-Lou again. More silence. Even the kids knew what an important moment this was: they understood all of the implications, without being told, and they too waited breathlessly.

Finally Jean-Lou shook his head and said, "Well there is a problem..." More silence. More tension in the room. More eyes on Steve. Jean-Lou shook his head again and said, "I don't know how we can get her out of where she is..."

A smile, a huge look of relief, from Steve. "Really? That's the problem?" His voice was almost squeaking with excitement. "If that's the problem, Jean-Lou, that is not a problem. I can worry about that...That is not a problem."

"I kept it for you, Steve," Jean-Lou said, "I always was keeping it for you."

And so we all trooped from the table to the garden, to look at the difficult position the *roulotte* was in. Indeed it was not an easy place to move it from, at the top of a steep little hill next to the house. But, as Steve had said, that was not really a problem.

Not if you were able to charm half the men of two villages to help you bring your beloved dream of a gypsy caravan back to your new dream home in France. The *vigneron* next door to Jean-Lou was charmed into loaning his forklift. Someone else offered the use of a flatbed truck. There were several long midday meals at which the men discussed the impossibility of the situation (the French always start from the position that any task is impossible, or at least *pas évident*). These long meals in the middle of the day were frustrating to the American, but he got the help he needed and without too much delay the impossible had been achieved. The *roulotte* was coaxed off of her position next to the Poisson family home, safely secured onto a flatbed truck, gently driven out of the gates, through the village of Loches, and back to Essoyes.

The *roulotte* was home again. And now we had a real home too.

Return to Essoyes

I have deliberately decided not to tell the story of how or why our marriage fell apart. It is a long and complicated story, it is a sad story, and it is not the one I want to tell, at least not now. To me, what is more interesting and more important than what Steve and I lost is what we have managed to retain despite the breakup—a deep, true, and abiding friendship, a more or less happy family, and even our dream home in Essoyes.

Eight years after we bought it, when Phineas had graduated from college, and Sam had completed his first year of college; and when the landlords of my rented place in Silver Spring had gone from being irresponsible and stingy to completely dishonest, I decided it was time for a change. ("Oops, we forgot to raise your rent six years ago, now you owe the landlady $4,000 in back rent," the property manager said. "Um, no, I will not be doing that," I replied.)

I reminded them that six years earlier, when they had first proposed a rent increase, I had pointed out all the many fundamental things about the place that needed fixing, some of them presenting health and safety issues. It probably was not even legal for them to be renting that house in the condition it was in. I reminded them that at that time they had first proposed a rent increase I had protested that the place was certainly not worth a penny more than I was already paying, and the property manager had actually agreed with me. "You're right," she said. "I'll speak to the landlady about this."

And that was the last I had heard. I continued to pay my rent on time every month for six more years without ever signing a second lease, mainly because I knew that we shouldn't really be living in a house in such bad condition. The windows were more like screens, which meant that in the winter the heating bills were astronomical even when the house was kept at an uncomfortably chilly temperature. There was mold in the basement, and exposed insulation. There were a lot of problems with that place.

But the house was spacious and filled with light; it looked over a creek and there were beautiful trees in the yard, and azalea bushes that bloomed every spring with no encouragement from me; it was in a safe and friendly neighborhood, not too far from Washington; and the well-worn and very stained carpets, once cleaned, were actually not such a drawback in a household that included two teenage boys and a dog, especially for someone (like me) who was perfectly capable of just not looking at the carpet, choosing instead to focus on the sunlight dancing on the walls and the leaves whispering in the breeze. The neighbors even actually *appreciated* the sounds of drumming coming from our basement. ("Is that your son?" someone would ask, and when I cautiously replied the first time, "Um, yeeessss.." the response was, "He's really good!")

So, the pluses outweighed the minuses. For the first few years we lived in that house, I was in a pretty fragile emotional state as our marriage was falling apart; it was inexpensive for the amount of space, by local standards, anyway; and I certainly didn't feel like moving anywhere. So we stayed.

But: it was also a dump. The landlady, at 80-something years, had flaming red hair and a piss-and-vinegar attitude. Word was that she didn't want to sell the house because she didn't want to pay the capital gains taxes she would have had to pay in the more than thirty years she had owned it. But she didn't want to pay for repairs or even general upkeep either. Once after a storm a *very large* branch from a tree that had fallen onto an extension to the house that was supported only by two-by-four stilts stayed there for more than a month until I finally threatened to call the county. Then her son, a surly, impolite man with a seemingly perpetual sneer came in his fancy car with a contractor to see what "all the fuss" was about. He did not notify me he was coming and he did not even ring the bell when they arrived. "Um, Mom? There are some men in our yard," Sam said.

On another occasion the landlady herself had showed up at the house, also unannounced, wanting to see the kitchen cabinets I had complained about. (They were wooden cabinets about forty years old, and so worn out that every time you opened a drawer, sawdust would go drifting down into the cupboards below.) She offered to replace the *top* of the cabinet which, while hardly beautiful, was not the problem at all. "No," I said. "It's not the top that needs replacing. It is the cupboards," and I showed her why. "You don't think I'm going to replace these cabinets for *renters*, do you?" she asked, fixing me with an intent stare from her very blue eyes.

So. Finally, with the threat of a lawsuit before me, I decided that this was a clear signal from the universe—well, really from my landlady—that it was time to go.

The question was *where* to go. I would have loved to return to Brooklyn, but I knew I couldn't afford to live in New York City anymore. Minnesota still felt like home to me, and always will, I think. But it didn't feel like the right place to go, not then. Maybe not ever. I didn't know. I wasn't sure.

We still had the house in Essoyes, the only house we had ever owned anywhere. Steve had been using it every summer, and I got there whenever I could, which hadn't been very much for a few years. Mainly because we weren't together anymore, it was looking like we might have to sell the place. We had bought it as a couple, we had bought it as a place for our family to call home. But that home had been broken apart. We were maintaining an unusually civil, even an unusually friendly, relationship after the first few agonizing years of our separation; in fact, we actually had managed to create a relationship that was better in many ways than the one we had had before. We had a deeper and better friendship, with more independence for him, and more respect for me.

But in the circumstances, holding onto the house in France was putting a strain on our finances, and making less and less sense, especially since nobody was even living there most of the time. We had tried renting it out, but renting out a country place in France from the United States is problematic even for people more experienced with doing that sort of thing than we were. It hadn't worked very well. And so there was a constant refrain coming from Steve about how we were going to have to "sell the place."

As I ruminated over all this, while packing up boxes, holding a series of yard sales, and hauling things away, I realized that if we *were* going to have to sell the place, I wanted to at least have a few months in which to enjoy it. Steve had spent a few months there during his sabbatical a couple of years earlier. "I'm an adjunct," I said to myself. "I don't need anyone to give me a sabbatical, I can just give myself one."

And so for a variety of reasons, personal, professional, and financial, I decided, in the spring of 2015, that it was time to return to Essoyes.

* * *

When my mother had died in 1990, she left behind a grieving family and also a house very full of what is most commonly and most succinctly, though not most elegantly, described as "stuff." Because my dad's health was not good—he had multiple sclerosis—my sister and I knew that he probably wasn't going to be able to stay in that house for the rest of his life. So we started almost immediately after my mom's death to discard, haul away, and otherwise dispose of the too-many things in it, layer by layer. The process took years to complete, working gradually the way we did. But that was the way to do it.

There was some tension at first: my sister, understandably, wanted to just get rid of most of what was there. My brother and I, for different reasons, wanted to go more slowly. But we worked it out. It was during the initial period of clearing things out that I had found the fragments of my grandmother's journal, and I wanted to be especially careful with written records, or any boxes or other containers in which written records might be found. There were a lot of them! So I told my brother and sister to please not throw out "anything—anything!—on paper." They exchanged a look, and then looked back at me, stonily. "Who's going to do it, then?" my sister asked. "I will," I said. "I promise. I will do it all. I will come here as often as I can, and I will work on it every time I'm here." "O-kay!" they said, exchanging another look, and shaking their heads. I didn't care. I knew they would honor their promise, and also that I would honor mine. I also knew it was a quixotic endeavor, and expensive, all that flying back and forth to Minnesota on a paper chase, and kind of ridiculous in many ways. But I was nonetheless devoted to it. Besides, I reasoned, it would give me more time with my dad. And it did.

As the process of going through all the things in the house continued, every time I was able to make it back to Minnesota from New York, I was frequently overwhelmed. There are so many areas of expertise that surface when someone is in the process of dismantling a home that's been lived in for a long time. How do you know which of the cups and saucers your mother collected are valuable antiques, and which are garage sale items? How do you know what to do with the toxic cleaning chemicals under the kitchen sink? How do you keep the fragile, hundred-year-old letters you find from completely disintegrating on your watch? Also, how do you deal with the surges of emotion, the bouts of sadness and depression that evoking all those memories can bring on, and the almost inevitable family tensions that arise in the process?

On one of the days when I had been reeling from one problem to the next, I took myself to the nearest bookstore, thinking that there must be a book to help people through this process. Surely I was not the first person to feel this way. What did other people do to cope with it? It would be so helpful to hear their stories.

But there was no such book.

I knew that Linda Hetzer, one of my colleagues in New York, was going through the same process with her father, on Long Island, and over a period of months we had casually exchanged a few commiserating remarks. The next time I saw her I asked her if she didn't think there should be a book about this topic: and she had had the same idea. We began to explore the idea together, of writing the book we thought people needed to help them through this process. The book was published in 2004, and it was called *Moving On: A Practical Guide to Downsizing the Family Home*, with a tag line that promised to help people figure out "How to Get Rid of the Stuff, Keep the Memories, Maintain the Family Peace, and Get On With Your Life."

Knowing that I was now engaged in the tedious process of figuring out what to do with all the stuff in my dad's home not merely as a bereaved daughter and frustrated seeker of my grandmother's journals, but as a *writer* suddenly made the process much less tedious and more interesting. Now I was doing research! Now I was able to look at it all through the eyes of potential readers: What did people need to know about this process? Who could help them? How could all this information be best arranged? It was still a pretty tedious task, and I still wanted to find my grandmother's journals, and be done with it: but turning the task into a professional activity made it a lot more rewarding.

The irony that it was my mother's aggravating, cluttering ways that had brought me to my first book project was not lost on me. Once the book was published and I was doing my round of promotional activities, I could just imagine her saying: "You see? I knew there was a good reason I was keeping all that stuff!"

And of course, it was in the process of going through all that stuff that I had found those few precious pages of my grandmother's journal that led me into the quest that eventually led to writing this book.

Now, eleven years after its publication, it was time to follow the advice in the book Linda and I had written together. The timing was not great, but it was feasible. I had twenty-three days to get everything out of that house in Silver Spring. I had to be teaching in Paris by July 1, and I had promised to take a friend to Essoyes for a couple of days before I started teaching; we would be flying to France together. On June 1 I gave notice to the property managers that I would be vacating the house on June 23. Then, in a wild flurry of activity, I went about selling, donating, and throwing out much of what was in that four-bedroom house, with a basement, and garage; threw (pretty much literally) what was left into a storage locker; and went to France.

I had no intention of staying there for longer than a few months in the beginning. I wasn't moving to Essoyes, or to France. I was just moving out of Silver Spring; that was the main thing at the time. I was just going to Essoyes to figure out what to do next.

* * *

That summer while I was teaching in Paris, Jeffrey Greene invited me to meet him for a drink at La Rotonde. He wanted to express his gratitude for my having used his book *French Spirits*, about his life in rural Burgundy, in my classes at Politics and Prose. He presented me with a signed copy of a collection of his poems. And when he asked me (casually, innocently) what I was doing now, I found myself spilling out much of the madcap adventure I had now embarked upon, scarcely knowing for sure exactly what I had done. He listened appreciatively, and then, when I paused and, embarrassed, apologized for giving **way** too long an answer to a fairly simple question, he just grinned and said, "Well. If you crash and burn, you crash and burn..." echoing his lively, indomitable mother's frequent mantra, a mantra I knew well from having read *French Spirits* several times.

In September I returned to Washington to connect with our boys, to see Phineas off for a year of teaching in France, and drive Sam to Oberlin for his second year of college. I taught a class at

Politics and Prose. And I went to the storage unit, where whatever I had saved from my hasty downsizing was now in boxes stacked too high and too tight to allow for easy access. I poked around in a few of them, the ones I could reach, and grabbed whatever I could find. I ended up finding my grandmother's diary from the years 1965-1969, and a small stack of postcards she had written to my mom in the 1940s. I packed them and brought them along with me to Essoyes, figuring that at least I could get those things read in the few months I would be there before I had to return to the US to apply for a visa.

* * *

Two snapshots from the first few weeks of my new life in France. On my way from Paris to Essoyes, driving a rental car, I stop at the Intermarché in Bar-sur-Seine to load up on a few staples I know I will need: long-conservation milk, toilet paper, boxed soups, wine. At the check-out, when my receipt is totaled a huge pile of colorful cardboard jetons comes spilling out of the change receptacle. The cashier scoops them up and hands them to me. I look at her blankly, jet lag exacerbating my confusion and delaying my return to being able to articulate myself in French."Alors, don-nez-les au monsieur," she says, taking them back and handing them to the man behind me in the line. Later I wonder what I missed winning, but to me it seems there has already been a poetic kind of justice. I have returned to France and this time I get to stay for a while. For me that is winning the jackpot.

A few weeks later I am returning to Essoyes alone, after having driven across France with Phineas to Toulouse, where he is working as a teaching assistant in a lycée professionel. It is dark when I arrive on an evening in early November. Typical of me, I have not thought ahead to how I will find my way through the trees to the house in the dark, and although there is in fact a bright little flashlight somewhere in my purse, at the time I am unaware of this fact. I stumble through absolute darkness in the general direction of the house. I can't see a thing. Eventually I realize that I am in front of the house, a good several meters away from the path that leads to the door. I find my way back to the path and finally find the light switch for the outdoor lights. It is the last time I will stumble toward the house in the dark. I will have become the kind of woman who has her flashlight ready when she needs it.

When Steve and I bought our place, a beautiful chalet on a spacious plot of wooded land, bordered by fields on one side, and forest on the other, with a lovely view of the village a kilometer away, I never imagined living there by myself. There is a lot of maintenance in any home, and this one had more maintenance than most, with a large yard, and a swimming pool. (We had had absolutely no idea how much maintenance swimming pools require, but we quickly learned. In the first couple of years we had the place Steve frequently quipped that we had bought "a swimming pool that came with a house.")

Steve was able to manage all that pretty well, even being there only a few months of the year: Steve is a sculptor, and he is very handy.

I am a writer: and although some writers are handy, I am most definitely not one of them.

So I wasn't going to Essoyes to live: I was only going there initially to figure out what to do next. However, once I got there, the feeling of deep contentment that overtook me was an unexpected and delightful surprise.

I do believe, generally speaking, that within reason happiness depends much more on a person's ability to be happy than on the circumstances of his or her life. There are of course events, and life passages that are going to be painful, where a person is bound to be unhappy for a while—the loss of a loved one, for example. The breakup of a marriage. A terrible illness. But other than these situations, or moments of crisis, I believe most happy people are happy because they know how to be happy, and they have learned how to not allow the inevitable frustrations, disappointments, and challenges of life to make them unhappy.

One of the greatest gifts my parents gave me, simply through the way they lived their lives, was the knowledge of how to be happy. And so, despite the difficulty of those eight years in Silver Spring when I was getting over the disappointment, grief, and heartache caused by losing Steve, I had been, after the first couple of extremely painful years, more or less happy. I enjoyed my work, I enjoyed my friends, I enjoyed having our kids spend most of their time with me. I enjoyed our neighborhood. I enjoyed the sunlight bouncing around that large, spacious, falling-apart house we were renting: I enjoyed my walks around the neighborhood, up hills and down, and the view from the window where I worked, that looked over a creek.

But during all that time, I had never experienced the kind of joy that I now felt in Essoyes every single day. A joy that bubbled up, unbidden, and caused me to whisper to myself, several times a day: "I'm so happy. I'm so happy. I'm so happy here!"

And so, I realized, Essoyes was where I was meant to be. At least for the time being.

Solitude without Loneliness

"**L**onesome. Nervous. Tired. And bored!"

These are the words I scrawled at the bottom of the page when I had finished recording my notes from reading those five years of my grandmother's diaries, from 1965-1969, during the first few months I lived in Essoyes.

It was hard to face this reality. Our family is a happy family, an uncomplaining family, a family that always makes the best of things. We are happy people!

And yet the evidence in these journals that my grandmother was not a very happy woman, at least late in her life, is pretty hard to avoid seeing.

She was seventy-three when she began this little book, in which she wrote *every single day,* without fail. Reading her diary was both physically tedious and emotionally difficult for me. First of all, her writing was very small and difficult to decipher. ("Why did she give herself only this much space?" was one of the first questions that occurred to me as I began reading.) She was not writing in an official diary, but in a little loose-leaf spiral notebook, 3 x 5 inches. She could have given herself as much space as she wanted to write each day, but she chose to write about each and every day of her life in a 1 x 3 inch rectangle, five years' worth of this recording of daily events, years stacked on top of each other, so that one could compare them, I guess, from year to year. But there was not much change from year to year.

This wouldn't have been so bad if what she had recorded had been more interesting, or if she had just been happier. What she had chosen to record was mostly the activities of her children and grandchildren, and the work she was still doing—cooking, cleaning, gardening, "putting up" food, mowing the lawn—most of which she did not seem to really enjoy, even the more creative tasks. ("2/21/69. Worked at setting up the warp on the loom again. Such a job! Is it worth it? My time is nothing. Red, white and blue warp this time.")

Occasionally she would backtrack to fill in the details of a day she had apparently not written about on the day itself. The most poignant of these, the full entry on October 28, 1968, was when she was seventy-six years old: "Must have been a blank day." Quite a few other entries came close to saying the same thing: "Just another day." "Elmer and I just lived another day." "Bruce and Brenda went to German Club. Plenty to do if you're young..."

And so it was tedious reading.

The only household task it was pretty clear she enjoyed was hanging clothes outside on the line to dry, something my mother also loved, and that I love too. After my mother died, I would hang the clothes I had washed for my dad out on the line even on freezing mornings, where they would dry in stiff blocks of color. It felt in some weird, stubborn, but deeply comforting way like I was keeping her alive a little bit longer.

* * *

I try not to think badly of my grandfather, but it's hard...

I'm thirteen years old and my mother and I are arguing about something. Because I am "talking back" my grandfather gives my mother a look and says slowly, menacingly, "Do you want me to take her over my knee?" My mother looks back at him and calmly, evenly says, "No. This is between me and Janet." In that moment I develop a deep disliking of my grandfather, and my relationship with my mother has been saved.

The glimpses of him that come through in my grandmother's writing haven't done much to make me feel any better about him. I do remember his jolly laugh, and his love of music, especially the anthem of the US Marines. But I also remember his obsession with watching professional wrestling on television. So when I came across my grandmother's reference to the day she was able to watch what *she* wanted to watch on TV, I felt the sense of liberation she must have felt that day. But I felt even more acutely aware of the closing in, the submitting to or at least tolerating in the background things she *didn't* want to watch, that must have been a much more significant, and constant, part of her life.

My grandfather worked hard too, chopping wood for their wood-burning stove, gardening, going to town to sell squash and potatoes from his truck. And he worked unbelievably hard at terribly nasty work in the tannery all those years during the Depression when he couldn't afford to farm. One of the few hidden facts about his life I managed to uncover somehow in the process of writing this book was the fact that he had lobbied for, and apparently succeeded in getting, showers installed for his fellow workers at the tannery. I didn't really understand the significance of this until a student in one of the writing workshops I was teaching read a description he had written about a visit to a tannery in Morocco. Hearing his vivid description of the scene—especially the stench—I knew that anyone who would try to get the management of a tannery to provide their workers with a shower at work so they could go home in a less disgusting condition, was probably essentially a good person.

But did my grandmother really have to work that hard? Did she really have to live out her elderly years feeling that she was in a harness? Was it just part of my grandparents' habit of living, one that they weren't able to let go of? Or perhaps part of the Puritanical necessity of feeling like a good, a worthy person?

I don't know. But I do know that as I read those tiny pages, a little bit at a time because it was too depressing to read them through all at once, I felt resentment, as well as sadness, on behalf of my grandmother. It seemed to me that she had been lonely, and unful-filled in some important ways.

Is that part of why she had the vision of her father, who had appeared to her one day? She had told my mother about this vision, about suddenly seeing her father, who had been long dead, standing outside her window, and about going outside to talk with him. It had been the most natural thing in the world, she said. But then just as suddenly as he had appeared, he was gone again. "I never thought to try to touch him," she told my mother. "I wish I had." She told my mother not to tell anyone else, lest she be thought crazy. But she wanted my mom to know, and apparently my mom wanted me to know too.

The laborious process of going through the letters and journals continued slowly, unsteadily, whenever I could. The process is much like panning for gold. Most of what you read is boring or irrelevant. It all drags you into an unsettling and unnerving, for me almost suf-focating, feeling of drowning in the past. But you can't stop, not if you want the answers to your questions. And so I kept on.

One day, at the end of a long day of tedious downsizing tasks, sorting through photos, jewelry (Is it costume? Is it real? I don't know, I don't care!), and letters, a few at a time, I thought I had struck gold: I found a letter to my mother that I thought was from one of her brothers, describing their mother's terrible state of mental illness, her commitment in the state hospital in Rochester, her suf-fering from electroshock treatments, his fear that she would be sub-jected to a lobotomy. Wow! I thought. I couldn't believe it.

I wrote to my cousin, cautioning her to receive what I was about to ask her in confidentiality; asking her if she had ever heard about Grandma being hospitalized for mental illness, not long before we were born. She had not. Did she think I should ask her mother, my Aunt Rose Ann, about it? And if so, could she prepare her for such a question coming to her, out of the blue? Yes, and yes.

Well, it turned out that the letter was *not* from my uncle, and had nothing to do with my grandmother at all. As it turned out, Grandma's hospitalization for mental illness had simply been a product of my overactive imagination trying to fill in the frustrating blanks in her story. However, in the conversations that ensued it came to light that my grandfather, toward the end of his life, had been "difficult," and had been put on medication that he was told was for his heart, but really was a sedative. Apparently my grandmother had turned to my aunt and uncle for help, reporting that he was being abusive toward her. ("When you say 'abusive' what do you mean?' I asked my aunt, a bit amazed that the conversation was heading into such unexpected territory. "Well, she didn't really say, but that is the word she used," was her answer.) The way they had handled the situation was to tell the family doctor about the problem, and then my aunt, uncle, grandmother, and the doctor had decided together that the best thing to do was to prescribe medication to "calm him down." "But whatever you do, don't tell him that's what it's for!" they had told the doctor. "That would really set him off."

* * *

My grandmother had clearly wanted more out of life, and in my opinion she had deserved more. Why couldn't she have been allowed, at least in those later years, to have indulged herself in reading the books she loved to read? Was she being kept from reading by my grandfather and his "keeping her at it?" All that canning and baking, cleaning and gardening, helping him mow the lawn? Or had she at some point along the way decided to keep *herself* from it? Maybe so, since in fairness to my grandfather I must admit that the reference to being "back in the harness" was made nearly a year after he had died.

The reserved, oblique, matter-of-fact way in which she recorded my grandfather's death seems notable. The entire entry reads: "November 28, 1967. It has happened!" A few months later, on their wedding anniversary, she wrote "48 years and I am alone." That is the full entry.

It may—or may not—also be notable that one of the more positive entries I found in all those five years occurred after my grandfather's death. Though she often wrote about the weather, she rarely mentioned the beauty of the landscape. But in May of 1969 she did mention the beauty of the lilacs and the azaleas, almost as if she were first waking up to them, or waking up to them again.

There were glimpses of another woman, of her earlier self, and of a more engaged connection with life in that little notebook covering five years; not many, but a few. On July 21, 1969, she wrote about the Apollo landing on the moon. "Man on the Moon! I washed [clothes] and watched TV, Channel 4. It surely was fine! They got back to Apollo safely. Holiday for Fed." Then, typically, without even a change of paragraph (no room for it, in that tiny little rectangle she was writing in!), she was back to her own life, or rather the lives of her grandchildren. "Leo is taking swimming lessons again this week..." But a few days later she was commenting on Apollo again: "The Moon Men are back. I cried when Nixon talked to them. And the prayer. Very impressive."

I wondered why she had even bothered to write. What was it for? *Who* was it for? I will of course never know the answer to these questions, but it seems fairly obvious to me that a large part of the reason may have been simply to keep herself sane, and to keep the loneliness at bay. She refers in a few places to writing letters, and how "letters [both written and received] help." Talking also helped. But it seems that she didn't have enough of the right kind of people to talk to. Even when she went for a long-awaited visit with her sister in 1969, after their first day together, when she noted that they had "talked about old times mostly," the next day she wrote, "Watched all the daytime TV stories [soap operas]," adding, "May likes them." In early July of that year, she recorded the arrival of a friend who had come to visit and noted, "We talked in the car for at least two hours..." How hungry she must have been for that conversation!

She was of course living in a world where the expression of emotion was not exactly encouraged, nor were intellectual pursuits. Had she internalized the values of that culture eventually, just given up? In her journal, even the potentially interesting stories are not really told, just alluded to in cryptic fashion. For example, in the summer of 1968, "Pastor talked about Chicago." (There were riots at the Democratic national convention in Chicago that year, but you wouldn't know it from her diary. Nor did she reveal what the pastor had said about Chicago.) Another entry alluded to "Disturbing news about Sandy." (She doesn't say what the disturbing news is, but several weeks later there is a baby shower, and her remark is "Everybody was sorry but made the best of it.") In another entry: "Went to see L. and she talked a lot about things on her mind." And so on.

Though by the time I was reading these journals I had become rather comfortable with the idea that I must have been mistaken in my childhood notion that my grandmother didn't like me, I couldn't help but feel as I read these journals that maybe I had been right about that after all. She had a clear preference for some of her granddaughters, and I did not appear to be one of them. The closest to a positive thing she said about me was written on Mother's Day in 1966, when I was thirteen. "Janet was so thrilled with the Punteney French descent," she wrote, referring to one of her ancestors. But was it really a positive comment? Or was it tainted with some kind of Midwestern notion about people who took on airs about being French? Unlike some of my cousins, I never came in for direct praise, even when she reported that I had gotten straight A's on my report card. (The fact was recorded, but there was no exclamation mark, and no further comment. A classic case of damning with faint praise?)

There is very little verbatim dialogue recorded in her diaries, but one of the few bits she did record is a comment a child she was babysitting had made. "This is a quiet house," the little girl had said.

"Yes, just a little girl and an old lady," my grandmother replied. "You're not an old lady, you're a teacher! You can teach anything!" the child had protested. This probably alluded to the fact that my grandmother had taught my cousins to play the piano, something this particular child would have had the chance to observe.

"Grandma was a good piano teacher," my cousin Brenda told me when I asked, and she remembers the day when she had told her, "I've taught you everything I know, you will have to find another teacher to work with you from here on." But she doesn't remember ever hearing my grandmother play the piano herself, for her own pleasure. She would have only been able to do so in my cousins' home, since she had given her piano to them so the kids could learn to play. But as a young woman she had played in concerts in Cresco: so this was one more avenue of creative expression silenced. Why?

She also once made note of finding an article for my cousin Bruce to refer to in one of his term papers. "So I can go to college with Bruce," she remarked. Clearly she had an unanswered hunger for knowledge, for a more intellectual life. So was she jealous of me, somehow? Is *that* why she didn't like me? Did she see me heading toward a future she had once seen for herself but hadn't been able to realize? And rather than experiencing vicarious pleasure from that, did she resent it?

I don't know! But if so, how sad that she couldn't have taken pleasure in thinking that maybe I would be able to escape the world that had cornered her and restricted her horizons. And even sadder the fact that she would never know, and probably could not have imagined, that one day one of the few admirers of her own literary creations would be this same granddaughter.

* * *

The place I have "run away" to, and where I feel more at home than anywhere else I have ever lived—except maybe Brooklyn—is not that different than the place my grandmother left when she married my grandfather and ran away from her home also. Essoyes is a small rural village surrounded by fields of grain planted in an open plain surrounded by gently rolling hills. When I take my daily walks across the field next to our home, except for the very French-looking village to my right and the vineyards in the distance, I could be in Iowa.

But I'm not. I'm halfway around the world from there, and in that simple fact lies so much of the reason that this place is, for me, liberating.

I know it's not necessarily liberating for the people who were born and raised here, many of whom will probably not ever go very far from here. For them Essoyes may be stifling, even suffocating. Or it may simply be comfortable, and it may be all they want. "Why move away from home and culture, from one's very language? What makes one person sit and the other wander? Why, in the same atmosphere can some breathe and others not?" Janet McDonald asked in her poignant, eloquent essay "X-Patriate," about the path that had taken her from her home in a Brooklyn housing project to her life as a lawyer and creative writer based in Paris.

The lay of the land in Essoyes is much the same as it is in Iowa, but the buildings and the culture are very different. Cresco, Iowa, wholesome and wonderful as it is in many ways—or at least as it seemed to be when I visited there in 2006—had, at least for me, none of the comforting sense of continuity that breathes from the very walls of Essoyes, those walls that give me such a feeling of joyful connection to the hundreds of years lived here as I walk by them on my way into town. Of course I know that many of the lives that have been lived within those walls have been far from joyful. War, foreign occupation, poverty, plague, all of these things have marked life here: I know that within these walls there has been much suffering, probably much more suffering than joy. Only recently in human history have people—and not even that large a percentage of people—been able to live their lives in relative safety and comfort, to even *think* about enjoying their lives, rather than just enduring them.

And yet, and yet. It is in part that sense of continuity, of ancient tradition shaping and informing modern life, subtly, elusively, but undeniably, that makes me so deeply contented to be here.

Cresco, Iowa is still a thriving small town whose future is probably relatively secure, as a county seat. But Bonair, the village where my grandmother was born and lived for the first nineteen years of her life, is not really a village anymore. It is a small grouping of homes in a place where there was once a lively little village with a church, a school, and a variety of local services. I don't know the people of today's Bonair, and I have never spent any time there, so I have no way of knowing whether it is a warm and friendly, tight-knit community, or a collection of isolated homes. I do know that the people who live there have to drive quite a way to avail themselves of any goods or services. There is no walking anywhere, except of course, across the glorious, open plains.

Essoyes on the other hand has, through all manner of ups and downs, survived and thrived. There are complicated reasons for why it has done so, and Bonair has not. The countries and the cultures in which these two villages are situated are different in some fundamental ways that have an effect.

I often think of Aline Charigot, the wife of Pierre Auguste Renoir, who was born and raised here, when I see young mothers pushing strollers around the village, looking bored, often smoking cigarettes. Aline Charigot grew up poor in Essoyes. Aline's mother, who was abandoned by her husband, struggled to survive. Like so many other poor women in rural France in the late nineteenth century, she left her baby with relatives and went to Paris, where she supported herself by working as a seamstress. And so mother and daughter were separated from each other until, at the age of fifteen, Aline moved to Paris to be with her mother and learn her trade. And it is there that, by a stroke of luck, Aline met Renoir, the painter who would change her life, and with whom she would achieve middle-class respectability and comfort.

It was Aline who brought Renoir to Essoyes, at first pleadingly. It was not easy to tear the painter away from Paris, where he had spent most of his life. But he came to love Essoyes as much as she did, maybe even more. *"Dans ce milieu favorable ou il trouvait le calme sans isolement et le recueillement sans mélancolie, il a peint un grande nombre de toiles,"* wrote his friend Georges Rivière. "In this good place, where he found peace without isolation and contemplation without melancholy, he painted a great many paintings."

Peace without isolation and the chance to contemplate without melancholy is not a bad way of describing what I have found in Essoyes too. And the chance to do my work.

EPILOGUE

*"IT TAKES THE WEALTH OF THREE GENERATIONS TO MAKE A MUSICIAN —
THE FIRST TO WORK THE FIELDS, THE SECOND TO GO TO SCHOOL,
AND THE THIRD TO MASTER AN INSTRUMENT."*

—YO YO MA

Living a Dream Deferred

Like many of my neighbors in Essoyes, I heat our home during the winter mostly with a wood-burning fireplace. So one of the first things I needed to do when I arrived in October 2015, ready to resume work on this book, was teach myself how to use the fireplace. And so early one morning I opened it up and looked at the ashes that needed to be cleared away before the first fire could be built: I found something to scrape them with, over the grate and into the ash bin. And the scraping sound that made brought me instantly—almost eerily—back to my childhood.

It's early morning and I am upstairs in my grandparents' home. Someone is restoking the fire. Safe and warm in my bed upstairs, I hear first that scraping sound, then footsteps; then I feel a draft of cold, fresh air coming in from the door and up the stairs. Next, the thump of firewood being dumped on the kitchen floor. And then, after a little while, the smell of woodsmoke and the crackling of the fire. That's when I know it's safe to get up.

"How do you *know* your grandmother wanted to be a writer?" my son (the more skeptical one) asked me one day. "I have evidence," was my reply. What I should have really said is, "Because I found her writing. And she *was* a writer. She just never had the chance to do very much about it."

What I meant is that I had evidence that she would have liked to do more with it. And I do. But the truth is, what I have is much more intuition than solid evidence. The trail is actually pretty weak, just bits and pieces that I have been able to capture out of the letters and journals I was able to find. An elusive phrase here, a chance fact there, put together with my own interpretation of these sparse clues, obviously subject to the same possibility for error that exists in any nonfiction work, especially memoir.

I think I've gathered enough evidence to suggest that my grandmother might have liked to be a writer. But she certainly never said as much, at least not to me. And that is one of the things I feel luckiest about—that my childhood fantasy of becoming a writer was encouraged to blossom and become a reality, while hers (if indeed she had one) faded away, was never even spoken of.

Could she have created a different fate for herself, found a place for herself on the East Coast, a place she saw as the place where people were able to speak English correctly without being seen as stuck-up? Maybe. Plenty of young women did, even back then, though fewer then than now.

As I continued to plow through all those letters, finally one day, several years after I had moved to France I found an interesting letter written by my grandmother to my mother.

Dear Carol,

I am having a hard time filling up this day. Maybe I can use up some of it writing to you. No special news…

You were wondering why I pushed you out so soon after you graduated from high school. Don't you think most of us can't see our own faults but try to avoid the ones our parents made? As a girl I lacked push myself but I always wished Mother had made me get an education but her idea was to get a job and that was what I did. I suppose it was alright, but for my children--Dad had no urge to send them beyond high school but I wanted them to at least have a chance to try earning their own way so it was up to them as far as finances but I would encourage as much as I could. So there you have it. A very simple explanation. Now then, all my mistakes that I am unaware of, you can avoid with your children. And the ones I can see, too. For they are many….

My grandmother had not gotten the education she would have liked to have. She had married my grandfather, who was a farmer. She had learned to raise chickens and turkeys. She had raised a family through the depths of the Depression; later she had made cross-stitched aprons for her granddaughters, and taught some of them (the ones with the patience to learn) how to tat. Her life had taken another course.

But she made sure that the mistake her mother had made—of not making sure that her daughter had an education—was not passed on to the next generation. And she had protected her children from the disdainful attitude my grandfather apparently held toward higher education.

My mother, in turn, had passed on to me not only the gift of the assumption that I would be well educated—but the additional belief that it was important to follow your dreams.

* * *

This story is the story of my grandmother, my mother, and me. But I like to think it is a broader story as well, a story not just about the deferment of a specific dream in one Midwestern family through three generations of women, but really a story of the slow but steady progress American women have made in gaining the ability to play a greater role in directing the course of their own lives over the past hundred years. It's the story of how in that delicate balance of strategy, effort, and luck that has an effect on all human lives, the role of circumstance and luck has become somewhat less dominant in defining women's lives, leaving more room for strategy and effort to take us where we want to go.

For me, the chance to return to Essoyes at this juncture in my life has meant the chance to enjoy this beautiful place, this dream home of ours, for a little bit longer. And to finish writing this story, which I began so long ago.

The ceramic "Little Homemaker" figurine that my grandmother gave ten-year-old me is with me now, after having spent several years in that storage locker in Maryland. She has a place of honor on top of one of my bookshelves, where she reminds me daily of my grandmother, and the critically important, but also mysterious role she has played in my life, especially in my life as a writer.

It has been the perfect time, and the perfect place, to begin to tell this story—and how my mother and my grandmother helped me be able to tell it.

Acknowledgements

A ny book is the result of a collaborative process, and this is one is no different. Many thanks to Ginnie Cooper, Dorothy James, Diane Johnson, Anne Kostick, Phineas Rueckert, Stephen Rueckert, Kevin Sisson, Darcy Trick, and Diane de Vignemont for reading drafts of this work and giving me very helpful feedback.

Thanks also to Tor and Siffy Torkildson for publishing an excerpt from "Back to Bonair" in *The Pilgrimage Chronicles: Embracing the Quest*. And a big, huge thanks to the whole team at BookBaby, especially to Matthew Idler who has guided me through the publication process twice now, both times with great patience, wisdom, enthusiasm, and skill. And to the design team for the beautiful cover. And to Steven Spatz for starting the whole thing, and for keeping it going: he has given so many fine writers the chance to see their books published on a reasonable timetable— and to retain a healthy measure of artistic and economic control over them.

Some of the people I want to thank go way back: Colleen Molitor, my childhood next-door-neighbor and lifelong friend, and Ulla Dannebom, neighbor and friend in Washington DC. They were the first really eager listeners to my stories (Ulla even presented me with some notes she had taken on some of the stories I had told her). And Bill Chamberlain, for giving me the courage to take that first trip to Europe; for encouraging me, for believing in me, and for teaching me how to trust my instincts as a reader, which is more important than one might think—at least it has been for me.

I also want to thank the people in Iowa who helped me get started on the research for this book: Anna May Davis of Lime Springs; Marian Anderlik and Mary Ann Billmyer of the Howard County

Historical Society, and Janice Sowers of the Howard-Winneshiek Genealogical Society; and the kind and helpful staff at the Cresco Public Library when I went there in 2006. Some of these people are no longer alive, but their dedication to preserving and sharing local history lives on.

Deep thanks also to Lawrence Jordan, Penelope Rowlands, and Elaine Showalter, whose belief in me and in the value of my work helped strengthen my own belief in it. And also to Susan Coll, Ellen Hampton, and Marybeth McMahon, for general good friendship and writerly support.

There are a few women who I think of as my "big sisters." They have each provided me with essential encouragement and support at key moments in my journey: Karen Fawcett, Cherie Hales, Beth Mann, Lynn Westrope.

Thanks also, and always, to my family: Mom, Dad, and BOTH Grandmas (!) And to Steve, Phineas, and Sam for neverending love, and for your support of and belief in this book. And to my cousin Brenda Singer, and my Aunt Rose Ann Powers, who helped me track down a few elusive details of the story that I couldn't have found any other way.

Finally, many, many thanks to *mi querida hermanita*, Elizabeth Hulstrand Sanchez, who has been such a wonderful sister to me in so many ways: and who is perhaps more eager than anyone else to hold this book in her hands. A thought that has kept me going, and made it finally happen.

Credits

The letters and journals quoted in this book are from the author's personal collection. In some cases the names of the authors of the letters have been changed (or omitted) to protect privacy.

All of the photographs are in the author's personal collection, and are credited as follows. Wherever possible, permission has been given to publish the photos in this book.

Dedication page: Author reading to her brother, c. 1960.
Photo by Carolyn Hulstrand.

Janet Hulstrand in Bonair, Iowa, 1992. Photo by Stephen Rueckert.

Ini Sanborn Griffith and Effie Sanborn.
Date and photographer unknown.

Bonair, Iowa Train Depot. Photo gift of Anna May Davis.
Photographer unknown.

Elmer and Effie Powers on their wedding day, 1920.
Photographer unknown.

Jim, Lewey, and Dave Powers, 1945. Photographer unknown.

Carolyn Powers with her brothers, c. 1930. Photographer unknown.

Carolyn Powers, nursing school graduation photo, c. 1945.
Photographer unknown.

Bert Hulstrand and Carolyn Powers, late 1940s. Photographer unknown.

Carolyn Hulstrand at Janet & Steve's wedding, 1985.
Photographer unknown.

Janet with her cousin Darlene, 1954. Photographer unknown.

School portrait of the author, 1960. Photographer unknown.

Portrait of the author on a boat, 1979. Photo by Stephen Rueckert.

Steve seen through the vines, 1978. Photo by Janet Hulstrand.

Portrait of the author on the Brooklyn Bridge, c. 1983.
Photo by Stephen Rueckert.

Family Portrait, 2000. Photograph by David Schroeder.

Selling Kool-Aid for the Kennedy Library, c. 1964.
Photo by Carolyn Hulstrand.

Author with Paul Robeson, Jr. and Lawrence Jordan.
Photo by Stephen Rueckert.

CUNY students in Paris. Photo by Janet Hulstrand.

The author with students at Politics and Prose, 2012.
Photographer unknown.

Our chalet in Essoyes, 2007. Photo by Stephen Rueckert.

La roulotte, 2007. Photo by Stephen Rueckert.

Portrait of the author in Essoyes (holding *baguette*) 2015.
Photo by Kevin Sisson.

The author in Essoyes, 2019. Photo by Stephen Rueckert.

Mementos from three generations of writers. Photo by Janet Hulstrand.

About the Author: Portrait of the author in Essoyes, 2015.
Photo by Kevin Sisson.

The following Iowa newspapers are quoted: the *Cresco Plain Dealer,* the *Howard County Times,* the *Lime Springs Sun.* I had access to them thanks to the Cresco Public Library. There is also a brief quotation from the January 15, 1964 *Cincinnati Enquirer,* quoting a letter I wrote to Jackie Kennedy in 1963.

Fragments or phrases from the following literary works are quoted, and the artists are here credited: Johnny Burke, from "Swingin' on a Star"; W.B. Yeats ("changed, changed utterly") from "Easter, 1916"; Joni Mitchell ("they paved paradise") from "Big Yellow Taxi"; Jack Kerouac, from *Satori in Paris;* Hjalmar Peterson, from "Nikolina"; Ernest Hemingway, quoting Evan Shipman in *A Moveable Feast;* James Baldwin, from "The Discovery of What It Means to Be an American"; E.B. White from *Here Is New York*; Janet McDonald from "X-Patriate," published in *The Literary Review;* Georges Rivière, from *Renoir et ses amis;* and Yo-Yo Ma, quoted in various places.

About the Author

Janet Hulstrand is a writer, editor, writing coach, and teacher. She grew up in Minnesota, and has lived in New York City and Washington DC. She created and has taught "Paris: A Literary Adventure" for City University of New York study abroad programs since 1997, and she teaches literature and culture classes for Politics and Prose bookstore in Washington. She writes frequently for *Bonjour Paris, France Today, France Revisited,* and for her blog, *Writing from the Heart, Reading for the Road.* She is the author of *Demystifying the French: How to Love Them, and Make Them Love You* and coauthor of *Moving On: A Practical Guide to Downsizing the Family Home.* She lives in Essoyes, a beautiful little village in the Champagne region of France, where she is working on her next book.